First Language English

for Cambridge IGCSE™

WORKBOOK

Graham Elsdon & Helen Rees-Bidder

Sixth edition with Digital access

Shaftesbury Road, Cambridge CB2 8EA, United Kingdom

One Liberty Plaza, 20th Floor, New York, NY 10006, USA

477 Williamstown Road, Port Melbourne, VIC 3207, Australia

314–321, 3rd Floor, Plot 3, Splendor Forum, Jasola District Centre, New Delhi – 110025, India

103 Penang Road, #05–06/07, Visioncrest Commercial, Singapore 238467

Cambridge University Press & Assessment is a department of the University of Cambridge.

We share the University's mission to contribute to society through the pursuit of education, learning and research at the highest international levels of excellence.

www.cambridge.org
Information on this title: www.cambridge.org/9781009528801

© Cambridge University Press & Assessment 2025

This publication is in copyright. Subject to statutory exception and to the provisions of relevant collective licensing agreements, no reproduction of any part may take place without the written permission of Cambridge University Press & Assessment.

First published 2002
Second edition 2006
Third edition 2010
Fourth edition 2014
Fifth edition 2018
Sixth edition 2025

20 19 18 17 16 15 14 13 12 11 10 9 8 7 6 5 4 3

Printed in Italy by L.E.G.O. S.p.A.

A catalogue record for this publication is available from the British Library

ISBN   978-1-009-52880-1   Workbook with Digital Access

Additional resources for this publication at www.cambridge.org/9781009528801

Cambridge University Press & Assessment has no responsibility for the persistence or accuracy of URLs for external or third-party internet websites referred to in this publication and does not guarantee that any content on such websites is, or will remain, accurate or appropriate. Third-party websites and resources referred to in this publication are not endorsed.

Cambridge International Education material in this publication is reproduced under licence and remains the intellectual property of Cambridge University Press & Assessment.

2024 Cambridge Dedicated Teacher Awards

Our **Cambridge Dedicated Teacher Awards** are an opportunity to show appreciation for the incredible work teachers do every day.

Thank you to everyone who nominated this year; we have been inspired and moved by all of your stories. Well done to all of our nominees for your dedication to learning and for inspiring the next generation of thinkers, leaders and innovators.

Congratulations to our winners!

Global Winner
South East Asia & Pacific
Sydney Engelbert
Keningau Vocational College, Malaysia

East Asia
Pengfei Jiang
Zhuji Ronghuai Foreign Language School, China

Pakistan
Saeeda Salim
SISA - School of International Studies in Sciences & Arts, Pakistan

South Asia
Meena Mishra
Dr Sarvepalli Radhakrishnan International School, India

Middle East and North Africa
Gina Justus
Our Own English High school- Sharjah-Girls, United Arab Emirates

Sub-Saharan Africa
Tajudeen Odufeso
Isara Secondary School, Isara Remo, Nigeria

Europe
Aynur Bayazit
Menekşe Ahmet Yalçınkaya Kindergarten, Türkiye

Latin America & the Caribbean
Ramon Majé Floriano
Montessori sede San Francisco, Colombia

North America
Marisa Santos
Seminole Ridge Community High School, United States

For more information about our dedicated teachers and their stories, go to
dedicatedteacher.cambridge.org

Endorsement statement

Endorsement indicates that a resource has passed Cambridge International Education's rigorous quality-assurance process and is suitable to support the delivery of their syllabus. However, endorsed resources are not the only suitable materials available to support teaching and learning, and are not essential to achieve the qualification. For the full list of endorsed resources to support this syllabus, visit www.cambridgeinternational.org/endorsedresources

Any example answers to questions taken from past question papers, practice questions, accompanying marks and mark schemes included in this resource have been written by the authors and are for guidance only. They do not replicate examination papers. In examinations the way marks are awarded may be different. Any references to assessment and/or assessment preparation are the publisher's interpretation of the syllabus requirements. Examiners will not use endorsed resources as a source of material for any assessment set by Cambridge International Education.

While the publishers have made every attempt to ensure that advice on the qualification and its assessment is accurate, the official syllabus, specimen assessment materials and any associated assessment guidance materials produced by the awarding body are the only authoritative source of information and should always be referred to for definitive guidance. Practice questions included in this resource have been written by the authors to align with accessibility best practice. This may differ to how questions appear in assessment. Our approach is to provide teachers with access to a wide range of high-quality resources that suit different styles and types of teaching and learning.

For more information about the endorsement process, please visit www.cambridgeinternational.org/endorsed-resources

Contents

How to use this series ... vi

How to use this book ... vii

Introduction ... viii

Unit 1: Reading skills and strategies ... 1
1.1 An introduction to reading skills ... 1
1.2 Reading strategies ... 2
1.3 Types of texts ... 5

Unit 2: Reading for comprehension ... 10
2.1 Focusing on vocabulary ... 10
2.2 Putting reading strategies into practice ... 12
2.3 Using your own words ... 14
2.4 Explicit and implicit meaning ... 16

Unit 3: Summary writing ... 21
3.1 Reading for ideas ... 21
3.2 Remodelling the text ... 24
3.3 Developing a coherent summary ... 27

Unit 4: Analysing and explaining writers' effects ... 32
4.1 Understanding meanings and effects ... 32
4.2 Language chosen for deliberate impact ... 35
4.3 Exploring figurative language ... 40
4.4 Explaining how writers achieve effects and influence readers ... 43

Unit 5: Extended response to reading ... 50
5.1 Conventions of text types ... 50
5.2 Evaluating and using ideas from a text ... 53
5.3 Developing ideas ... 56

Unit 6: Reading practice ... 59

Unit 7: Writing skills ... 71
7.1 Content and style ... 71
7.2 Text structures ... 75
7.3 Word and sentence choices ... 77

Unit 8: Directed writing ... 80
8.1 Evaluating views ... 80
8.2 Responding to a task ... 84
8.3 Presenting your views ... 87
8.4 Writing letters and reports ... 89
8.5 Writing a speech ... 92

Unit 9: Descriptive writing ... 98
9.1 Describing places ... 98
9.2 Describing details ... 101
9.3 Using the senses ... 103
9.4 Describing events ... 106
9.5 Describing people ... 108
9.6 Improving descriptive writing ... 110

Unit 10: Narrative writing ... 113
10.1 Story elements and ideas ... 113
10.2 Story openings ... 115
10.3 Characterisation ... 117
10.4 Improving narrative structure ... 120
10.5 Refining your storytelling ... 121
10.6 Endings ... 124

Unit 11: Writing practice ... 126

Glossary ... 129

Acknowledgements ... 130

CAMBRIDGE IGCSE™ FIRST LANGUAGE ENGLISH: WORKBOOK

> How to use this series

This suite of resources supports students and teachers following the Cambridge IGCSE™ and IGCSE (9–1) First Language English syllabuses (0500/0990). All of the components in the series are designed to work together and help students develop the necessary knowledge and skills for this subject.

The Coursebook is designed for students to use in class with guidance from the teacher. It is divided into two parts: reading and writing, and provides lots of opportunities for students to develop these key skills through a range of engaging activities. Speaking and Listening tips offer different strategies to support students in enhancing these skills, while Reflection and Self-assessment features encourage students to think about their own learning. Each unit ends with a Project and Practice questions that help consolidate learning.

A digital version of the Coursebook is included with the print version and is also available separately.

The write-in Workbook consolidates the learning in the Coursebook by providing opportunities for more focused practice. It can be used flexibly as an additional resource to support learning in the classroom or at home for individual work. The Workbook fully reflects the structure of the Coursebook, making it easy to navigate. A digital version of the Workbook is included with the print version.

The Digital Teacher's Resource provides everything teachers need to deliver the course. It is packed full of useful teaching notes and lesson ideas, with suggestions for differentiation to support and challenge students, ideas for assessment, homework and project guidance.

A wide range of additional content, such as worksheets, PowerPoint slides, end-of-unit tests, and answers to Coursebook and Workbook questions, is also available to help teachers save time and enrich their practice.

> How to use this book

Throughout this book, you will notice different features that will help your learning. These are explained below.

LEARNING INTENTIONS

Each unit begins with a set of learning intentions to explain what you will learn in the unit.

KEY TERMS

Key vocabulary is highlighted in the text when it is first introduced. An accompanying definition is given in the margin to tell you the meanings of these words and phrases. You will also find definitions of these words in the Glossary at the back of this book.

LANGUAGE FOCUS

This feature focuses on the main grammar or language topics within a unit. It helps to deepen your understanding and knowledge of key concepts.

Exercises

These help you to practise skills that are important for studying Cambridge IGCSE First Language English. There are two types of exercises:

- Exercises that let you practise the Reading and Writing skills you have learnt.
- Review exercises that bring together skills learnt in the corresponding unit, pushing your skills further.

Practice questions

Units 2–5 in the Reading section and 7–10 in the Writing section contain some practice questions, which are identified throughout the units. These questions have been written by the authors and provide practice at responding to the type of task required by the syllabus.

Practice units

Units 6 and 11 provide you with a full set of practice questions similar to those you may see in an assessment.

Question 1

a   Give **two** examples of the types of chemicals used in junk foods, according to paragraph 1.

.... [1]

b   Using your own words, explain what Text A means by:

i   'large quantities' (line 2)

....

.... [2]

ii   'easily accessible' (line 7)

....

.... [2]

c   Re-read paragraph 2 ('Junk foods are appealing . . . low incomes.').

Give **two** reasons for young adults relying on junk foods.

• ....

• .... [2]

Question 1

a   Re-read this extract from **Text A**.

'When used appropriately, AI can supplement the work teachers do. It can be used to spot patterns in a student's work, identify common errors, design a suitable set of exercises to help them and then reassess in real time. It can even write full textbooks targeted at individual students, or design new exam papers and model answers. AI could be especially helpful for students with specific needs and challenges for whom teachers don't always have the time in a crowded day to provide one-to-one assistance.'

Use your own words to evaluate the writer's attitude towards the use of AI in schools. Give details from the text to justify your answer. [5]

> Introduction

The information in this section is based on the Cambridge International Education syllabus. You should always refer to the appropriate syllabus document for the year of examination to confirm the details and for more information. The syllabus document is available on the website: www.cambridgeinternational.org.

This write-in Workbook is designed to help you develop your skills in Cambridge IGCSE and IGCSE (9–1) First Language English syllabuses (0500/0990) for examination from 2027. A digital version of the Workbook is included with the print version.

It supports the Cambridge IGCSE First Language English Coursebook and fully reflects the structure of the Coursebook. This resource offers complete flexibility in how it is used – it may be used in class to supplement and consolidate learning in school or used as part of homework for further practice.

The content of this Workbook follows the same unit structure as the Coursebook, starting with Reading and then moving into Writing. This workbook offers plenty of activities and tasks to help enhance the skills that are central to the syllabus.

We hope you enjoy working through the tasks and exercises in this book!

Priya Govindan

Commissioning Editor, Cambridge University Press and Assessment

> Unit 1

Reading skills and strategies

> **LEARNING INTENTIONS**
>
> By the end of this unit, you will be able to:
> - identify how reading skills are used in everyday life
> - read actively
> - understand different reading strategies
> - identify the features of different types of fiction and non-fiction texts.

1.1 An introduction to reading skills

1   Read Text 1.1 and answer Questions a–c using any reading strategies you know.

Text 1.1

> There is no doubt that zoos are a hugely popular attraction for both adults and children, but is it morally right to keep wild animals in captivity?
>
> Supporters of zoos argue that they play a crucial role in educating people about the importance of conservation, and also inspire and encourage people to protect wild animals and their natural habitats. Many zoos provide a safe environment for endangered species and operate successful breeding programmes. Some zoos also rescue animals that have been mistreated or cannot survive in the wild due to health issues, or because they have been tamed from birth.
>
> On the other hand, those opposed to zoos argue that animals suffer both physically and mentally in captivity because they lack the space and freedom they would enjoy in their natural habitats. Many animals exhibit behaviours related to stress. Some animal parks force animals to behave unnaturally – by performing 'tricks' for the public, for example. Many of them have much shorter life expectancies than their counterparts in the wild. Critics also argue that breeding programmes rarely release animals into the wild, but instead sell animals to other zoos, or even to animal parks where people will pay a lot of money to hunt them.
>
> So, are zoos morally justifiable? You decide.

a Are the following statements true or false, according to Text 1.1?
Circle (◯) T (true) or F (false).

    i Zoos offer wild animals a better environment than their
natural habitats.   T / F

    ii Zoos help save endangered species.   T / F

    iii Animals that perform for the public live longer than in the wild.   T / F

    iv Some animals need to live in captivity.   T / F

    v Breeding programmes always lead to greater numbers of wild animals.   T / F

b Does the writer convey a viewpoint in this text?

....

c Make a list of the main points for and against zoos.

For:

....

....

....

Against:

....

....

....

1.2 Reading strategies

2 Text 1.2 is an extract from an article about food labelling. **Scan** the text to find the information you need to answer the following questions.

> **KEY TERM**
>
> **scan:** to read a text quickly to locate specific information in it

    a Why does the writer use the word 'scandal' rather than the word 'problem' in paragraph 1?

....

....

    b Explain the meaning of 'dangerous to consume' in paragraph 1.

....

    c Explain the meaning of 'bear no relation to' in paragraph 1.

....

d Give two reasons for using sell-by dates, according to paragraph 1.

- ....
- ....

e Give two examples of how consumers can use their senses to detect whether food is safe to eat, according to paragraph 2.

- ....
- ....

f Identify a word in paragraph 3 that means the same as 'approximately'.

....

g Identify a word in paragraph 3 that means the same as 'random'.

....

Text 1.2

> Supermarkets have come under pressure to resolve the scandal of waste caused by unnecessary and unrealistic 'sell-by' or 'best before' dates on food. The majority of consumers mistakenly believe that the dates on food packaging indicate when foods become inedible or dangerous to consume. But the truth is that these dates are unregulated, non-standardised and bear no relation to food safety at all. 'You may as well pluck a date out of thin air,' one consumer trading standards officer told us. Some dates relate to when a product is likely to be at its best quality. Others are intended as a guide, so stores know when to remove products from the shelves to alternate stocks.
>
> According to nutrition experts, sell-by dates do not ward off risks in terms of bacterial illnesses from consuming rotten food, because there are usually clear indications of mould or rot that can be seen by the naked eye or detected through smell or taste. Despite this, most consumers rely on sell-by dates rather than their own senses when deciding whether to use a food item, as they believe they are official safety guidance.
>
> This haphazard approach results in massive food waste. In the USA, for example, more than 80 million tonnes of food are wasted annually, which amounts to roughly a third of the country's food supply. According to the United Nations, 17% of global food production is wasted each year, at a cost of $680 billion. The majority of this is fresh, nutritious food, such as fruit and vegetables. This wastes energy in the form of the land, water and labour used to produce the food, as well as increasing greenhouse gas emissions when it ends up in landfill.

Some experts believe that the real problem lies in the fact that we have become 'disconnected' from our food sources, to the extent that we have lost confidence in our ability to decide whether something is edible or not. We don't know when a product was picked, who picked it, how it has travelled to us, or how long it has been on a shelf, so we put our trust in a wrapping of cellophane and a sticker bearing a date. That gives us meaning, despite having no idea what the date actually stands for.

3   Re-read Text 1.2 closely to gain a fuller understanding of it. As you read, make notes around the text, identifying any interesting features of the writing and any questions you have. Reading the text aloud may help you gain a fuller understanding of the features of the writing.

LANGUAGE FOCUS: IMPLYING AND INFERRING

In reading tasks, you may come across the terms 'imply' and 'infer'. They have related meanings, but they are not the same thing.

- To **imply** means to suggest something in an indirect way, without stating it explicitly.
- To **infer** means to work out a meaning by applying evidence and reasoning.

You can think of it in the following way: a writer implies something; a reader infers it.

Look at this sentence:

- 'As he watched, Radu's face turned increasingly red and he started to clench his fists tightly.'

As a reader, you might infer that Radu is becoming angry by what he can see. You have not been told this directly, but you have picked up on what the writer has implied here by their choice of language.

KEY TERMS

imply: to suggest something in an indirect way, without stating it explicitly

infer: to work out a meaning by applying evidence and reasoning

4   Read Text 1.2 inferentially, then answer the questions.

   a   What can you infer about shops' use of sell-by dates from the information in paragraph 1?

   ....

   ....

   ....

1 Reading skills and strategies

b What does the writer imply about people's knowledge of food safety in the line 'most consumers rely on sell-by dates rather than their own senses'?

....

....

....

c What does the writer suggest about the long-term impacts of food waste on the environment in paragraph 3?

....

....

....

d What can you infer about the writer's attitude towards mass-produced food from the assertion that people have become 'disconnected' from the sources of their food?

....

....

....

1.3 Types of texts

5 Read Extracts A–F. Complete Table 1.1 to identify the text type and whether it is fiction or non-fiction. Then, identify the purpose and audience of each text and explain your decisions by noting the features of each text.

> ### Extract A
> There was an eerie whisper of wings as the army of bats swooped over the dense canopy of trees. The castle loomed high on the hill as they swarmed towards it like an unstoppable sea. On the castle walls, the king's regiment stood firm, watching the dark cloud approach. There was no way they could defeat this enemy swooping in from above – but they were definitely going to try!

Extract B

My first memory is of taking a walk with my mother. We lived in the rural south then, long before we moved to the city for my father's job. She used to take me walking in the cornfield, where the crops grew so high that they were taller than me. It was during those walks that my mother impressed upon me that I could be anything or anyone. That woman made me the man I am today, and I owe my success to her.

Extract C

Many first-time parents express concern about whether their baby's sleep patterns are normal, or whether they should be encouraging longer intervals between feeds. The general response is that no individual baby is the same as another, so unless there are other concerns relating to sleep, parents should allow their baby to establish their own routine.

Extract D

There have been widespread protests throughout the county about plans for a new eight-lane highway linking residential areas in the south with the new industrial parks in the north. One resident told us that a compulsory purchase order for her property would leave her out of pocket, as none of the moving costs would be covered. She also stated that she didn't want her home to be bulldozed due to the precious memories of her parents and grandparents who had lived in the house before her.

Extract E

For a great city break, you can't go wrong with Beijing – the bustling capital of China. There is so much to see and do, not to mention the incredible array of food on offer. With its modern and comprehensive metro system, it's easy to get around quickly and cheaply, so you can create a completely personalised itinerary for your stay.

Extract F

The emperor appeared on the golden terrace far above the throngs below and slowly raised his arm into the air. As the crowds silenced and focused their eyes on him as one being, the atmosphere became grave and tense. What had he gathered them here to announce? A ripple of fear ran through the people – his people – as he opened his mouth to speak.

Extract	Text type	Fiction (F) or non-fiction (NF)	Purpose and audience	Reasons for your decisions
A				
B				
C				
D				
E				
F				

Table 1.1

CAMBRIDGE IGCSE™ FIRST LANGUAGE ENGLISH: WORKBOOK

6 Summarise what each text is about in one or two sentences.

Extract A:

....

....

Extract B:

....

....

Extract C:

....

....

Extract D:

....

....

Extract E:

....

....

Extract F:

....

....

7 Answer the following questions.

    a Why does the writer use the word 'swarmed' instead of 'flew' in Extract A?

    ....

    ....

    ....

    b Identify a phrase that means the same as 'persuaded' in Extract B.

    ....

    ....

    c Explain the meaning of 'express concern' as used in Extract C.

    ....

    ....

    d Explain what the writer means by 'leave her out of pocket' in Extract D.

    ....

    e Explain the meaning of 'incredible array' as used in Extract E.

    ....

    f Using your own words, explain three ways that the writer shows the power of the emperor over his people in Extract F.

    ....

    ....

    ....

    ....

> Unit 2

Reading for comprehension

LEARNING INTENTIONS

By the end of this unit, you will be able to:

- use different strategies to build vocabulary through reading
- understand how to respond to a variety of comprehension questions
- select appropriate information from texts for different purposes
- explain meanings in texts in your own words
- identify explicit and implicit meanings in a variety of texts.

2.1 Focusing on vocabulary

1 Rewrite sentences a–e by replacing the following words (in bold in the sentences) with words with the same meaning:

enormous   unfamiliar   loved   thought about   building

   a   The **enormous** branches of the tree shook violently as the wind roared through the forest.

   ....

   b   I found myself wandering cluelessly through the **unfamiliar** streets on the other side of the city.

   ....

   c   He simply **loved** the new bicycle his parents gave him for his fifth birthday.

   ....

   d   With one foot on the starting block, her heart pounded in her chest as she **thought about** her chances of winning.

   ....

   e   The **building** of the new house on the corner was progressing well; the windows had started going in.

   ....

2 Look at the words from Text 2.1 listed in Table 2.1. Complete the table to identify each word's meaning in context, synonyms and what the writer is conveying.

Text 2.1

> It was a gloriously sunny day, but the **gentle** breezes were cooling the air, so the heat was comfortable and **soothing** rather than **oppressive** as it usually was at this point in the summer. The children were **permitted** to play in the garden, although their mother had warned them not to go near the fishpond. The water was **stagnant** and full of weeds, making it dangerous and **unpleasant**. There was also a disgusting **stench** lingering in the air around the pond, as if something was rotting and **putrid** in the reeds **bordering** the water.

Word	Meaning in context	Synonyms	What the writer is conveying
gentle			
soothing			
oppressive			
permitted			
stagnant			
unpleasant			
stench			
putrid			
bordering			

Table 2.1

3 In your notebook, write a new sentence for each word listed in Table 2.1 to show you understand its meaning.

2.2 Putting reading strategies into practice

4   Read Text 2.2, then answer Questions a–i to practise using reading strategies, such as pre-reading, **skimming** and scanning. Before you answer each question, decide:

- whether it requires you to answer in your own words
- how detailed your answer needs to be.

> **KEY TERM**
>
> **skimming:** to read a text quickly to get a general overview of the topic and content

Text 2.2

Sea turtles have been in the oceans for over 100 million years, and they belong to one of the oldest reptile groups in the world – no wonder they are sometimes referred to as 'the dinosaurs of the sea'! They can be found residing in most of the world's oceans, apart from in polar regions. Adult male turtles never leave the water, but the females venture ashore to lay eggs – usually on the same sandy beach where they themselves hatched. After hatching, the baby turtles immediately make their way to the ocean, although a large proportion don't make it for a variety of reasons.

Turtles play a significant role in the ocean food web, as they feed on more than 200 types of vertebrates and invertebrates, including a lot of fast-growing sea sponges. This helps to protect coral reefs, providing essential habitats and food for many other sea creatures. They also help to maintain seagrass meadows by grazing on them and preventing the grass from growing too long. Healthy seagrass beds are a nursery ground for a number of marine species, as well as an important source of oxygen. Some species of turtle eat jellyfish, which prey on fish eggs and larvae and are therefore responsible for depleting fish stocks that feed other animals in the food chain, as well as humans.

Adult turtles can face dangers in the sea. For example, they may become entangled in shrimp nets and fishing lines. They are also susceptible to the damaging effects of plastic in the oceans, either by consuming microplastic particles or by swallowing larger pieces of plastic debris – mistaking them for food sources. They even get tangled up in plastic nets drifting in the shallow waters or that are washed up on the shoreline.

There are additional threats to the turtle population due to human interference during the nesting season. Poachers take and sell eggs on the black market as they are considered an edible delicacy. In some locations, tourists interfere with nests through ignorant and thoughtless behaviour, or try to 'help' hatchlings on their way to the sea.
Coastal developments can also destroy nesting beaches and can lead to artificial light spills on beaches which negatively impact the navigational skills of hatchlings. Human actions such as littering also have a significant impact on the survival chances of hatchlings, as they can become disorientated by discarded items as they make their way to the sea.

2 Reading for comprehension

a Why are sea turtles sometimes referred to as 'the dinosaurs of the sea', according to paragraph 1?

....

....

b Identify a word in paragraph 1 that means the same as 'travel'.

....

c Explain the meaning of the phrase 'variety of reasons' as it is used in paragraph 1.

....

d What is significant about the beach where female turtles generally lay their eggs, according to paragraph 1?

....

....

e How do turtles help the food chain by eating sea sponges, according to paragraph 2?

....

....

f Explain two ways in which seagrass beds are beneficial for marine life, according to paragraph 2.

....

....

g Give two ways that plastic can harm sea turtles, according to paragraph 3.

....

....

h Explain the meaning of 'human interference' as used in paragraph 4.

....

....

i   Suggest three ways in which tourism makes it more difficult for hatchlings to survive.

   ....

   ....

   ....

2.3 Using your own words

> **LANGUAGE FOCUS: CHOOSING SYNONYMS**
>
> When choosing your own words, remember that not all synonyms have exactly the same meaning. Be sure that your choice of words accurately reflects what that writer says or means.
>
> Look at this example:
>
> - 'they can become disorientated by discarded items as they make their way to the sea'.
>
> If asked to explain this in your own words, the meaning of 'discarded' would need to make it clear it refers to something that has been carelessly thrown away. Synonyms such as 'dumped' or 'abandoned' would work, but words such as 'rejected' or 'trashed' would not convey the exact meaning of the word in context, despite being listed as synonyms of 'discarded'.

5   Read the following sentences. Circle (◯) the best synonym from each list to replace the word in brackets, without altering the meaning of the sentence.

   a   He watched (open-mouthed) as the ball soared through the air and landed in their goal – they had won!

   shocked   speechless   amazed   dazed   aghast

   b   It was unfortunate that the weather was so unseasonably (humid); she could feel her clothes clinging to her uncomfortably.

   oppressive   muggy   damp   suffocating   wet

   c   She loved the new house with its (fresh) renovation and sparkling windows.

   modern   unorthodox   original   natural   unusual

   d   The party was in full swing, with too many guests (crammed) into the tiny apartment.

   forced   crowded   overloaded   rammed   crushed

2 Reading for comprehension

6 Fill in the gaps in this paragraph. Choose the most interesting or powerful synonyms of the words in brackets that you can think of. When you have finished, read the text aloud to check the words added read fluently with no awkwardness. Then make any corrections necessary.

The elderly gentleman .... (walked) into the room,

his .... (skinny) legs barely able to support him.

His face was pale and .... (thin) and his clothes were

.... (untidy). The room had the ....

(smell) of neglect, and newspapers were ....

(thrown) around the floor untidily. He looked ....

(very tired) and .... (unstable) on his feet.

He finally .... (sat) in the chair and closed his eyes.

7 Rewrite the following sentences, using your own words as far as possible.

   a The erosion of the coastal defences on the east coast meant that several residential properties were tottering precariously on the top of the cliff.

   ....

   ....

   ....

   b The monotonous grey tower blocks loomed above the network of narrow streets.

   ....

   ....

   c As the sun climbed higher in the sky, its pulsing rays became insufferable, and she had to seek shade.

   ....

   ....

   ....

   d The ocean liner was like a floating mountain, completely dominating the tiny port in which it was docked.

   ....

   ....

   ....

8 Answer these questions based on Text 2.2.

    a Using your own words, explain how plastic is harmful to sea turtles, according to paragraph 3.

....

....

....

    b Using your own words, explain what avoidable problems can make it more difficult for hatchlings to make their way to the ocean, according to paragraph 4.

....

....

....

2.4 Explicit and implicit meaning

9 Look at the sentences in Table 2.2. For each sentence, add a tick in the Explicit or Implicit column to show whether it offers explicit or implicit information to the reader. Explain your reasoning.

Sentence	Explicit	Implicit	Explanation
She hated the dress because the style didn't suit her and it was a bright colour.			
As she appeared on the stage she smiled widely, but she lacked her usual enthusiasm for the huge crowd in front of her.			
As he saw her appear in the distance, he frowned momentarily before calling out her name to attract her attention.			
The room was extremely messy, with discarded clothes all over the floor and drawers spilling out their contents.			
The car had seen better days and was getting expensive in terms of repairs, but she just couldn't let it go, as it once belonged to him.			

Table 2.2

10 Write the following command and question words in Table 2.3 to show whether they are more likely to be used when testing explicit or implicit understanding.

Explain   Identify   Describe   Give   Analyse   Outline

Assess   Consider   Evaluate   Justify   Suggest

Explicit	Implicit

Table 2.3

Practice questions

11 Read Text 2.3, then answer the questions.

Text 2.3

> A drone – a fantastic technical toy or a dangerous weapon? Although sold in most toy stores, drones are far from being a plaything. Drones are highly advanced machines that can fly at speeds of 100 km an hour, with large spinning blades and usually a complete amateur at the controls! A recipe for disaster in the opinions of many.
>
> The popularity of drones is increasing exponentially, but regulations controlling their use are lagging feebly behind. Flying a drone can be done as either a hobby or for professional use, enabling users to capture stunning images and films. However, both types of users can put others at risk, both directly and indirectly, as well as deliberately or accidentally.
>
> Collisions are the largest risk factor. Drones are often employed to capture images and film footage in crowded spaces such as festivals, marches and other large-scale events. They can also be a distraction for those driving or operating industrial vehicles. Even lightweight drones can cause significant damage to people or property. Drones flying too close to buildings and transport, such as helicopters and aeroplanes, can cause serious accidents.

Drones can easily be mounted with cameras and microphones, so they may be used for deliberate invasions of privacy or inadvertently pick up footage that infringes personal privacy. Both are violations of current privacy laws, but are a grey area in many cases at the moment. They could also be used for domestic or industrial spying by flying over private land and properties without the owner's consent. With little regulation, their operators are almost impossible to trace.

More research is needed on the potential impact of drones on aircraft engines. Tests are routinely applied for bird airstrikes but not for drones, yet a drone can be heavier than a Canada goose, a breed which has been known to completely destroy a jet engine in the occurrence of a bird strike. Drones have also been used to disrupt airport activity. For example, at Gatwick Airport in the UK in 2018, a drone operator played cat and mouse with the authorities for three days, grounding hundreds of flights and diverting landings to other airports. A signal jamming system around airports is too risky, as it could inadvertently block other critical communications endangering safety.

At present, drones are reasonably contained, but this is largely due to their own design limitations. Most can only fly for up to 30 minutes without needing recharging, and need to stay within a few hundred metres of the controller due to the limited range of wi-fi and Bluetooth. Until drones become more aerodynamic and, hence, faster, batteries get lighter and signal ranges extend, this is unlikely to change. However, regulations need to stay one step ahead rather than two steps behind, as they are currently. Governments need to act before disaster strikes!

2 Reading for comprehension

a Give two facts about drones from paragraph 1.

.... [1]

b Use your own words to explain what the writer means by the following phrases:

i 'highly advanced'

.... [2]

ii 'complete amateur'

.... [2]

c Re-read paragraph 2 ('The popularity . . . accidentally.'). Give **two** problems associated with the increased use of drones identified by the writer.

• ....

• .... [2]

d Re-read paragraph 3 ('Collisions . . . serious accidents.'). Identify **two** ways in which drones can cause accidents.

• ....

• .... [2]

e Re-read paragraphs 4 and 5 ('Drones can . . . endangering safety.').

i Explain why the writer is concerned that drones could be used to invade people's privacy.

....

....

.... [3]

ii Explain why drones threaten the safety of air passengers.

....

....

.... [3]

f Re-read paragraph 6 ('At present . . . disaster strikes.').

i Why does the writer use the word 'strikes' instead of 'happens' to describe a potential accident involving a drone?

....

.... [2]

ii Explain what the writer suggests about the rules of drone ownership and use in the phrase 'regulations need to stay one step ahead rather than two steps behind'.

....

....

....

....

....

.... [3]

12 What is the writer's attitude towards the current regulations for using drones? Use three details from the text to support your answer.

....

....

....

....

.... [5]

13 a Identify a word or phrase from Text 2.3 which suggests the same idea as the words written in bold: 'multiplying rapidly' and 'the most dangerous aspect'.

i   Drone sales are **multiplying rapidly**.

.... [1]

ii The risk of drones colliding with other objects is **the most dangerous aspect**.

.... [1]

b Using your own words, explain what the writer means by the words 'avert', 'major' and 'ignorant' (in bold) in the following extract.

'Governments all over the world need to act fast to **avert** the risk of a **major** incident caused by a criminal, reckless or **ignorant** drone operator.'

i   avert .... [1]

ii major .... [1]

iii ignorant .... [1]

> **Unit 3**
Summary writing

> **LEARNING INTENTIONS**
>
> By the end of this unit, you will be able to:
>
> - read a text and offer an overview of it
> - identify the main ideas in a text
> - differentiate between main ideas and supporting details or examples
> - reorganise and synthesise ideas
> - remodel a text in your own words
> - produce a coherent piece of new writing in response to a given task.

3.1 Reading for ideas

Read Text 3.1. Then answer the Task 3.1 questions that follow.

Text 3.1

> I feel so lucky to have gone through life as an identical twin and wouldn't change it for the world. My twin is my best friend and has been by my side for my whole existence. We were the only twins in our year at school and always felt special – it was cool to have a best friend to go home with every night! As a twin, you don't have to figure out how to establish and navigate close relationships with others because it comes naturally. I have always instinctively known how to be a good friend, and how to compromise and make adjustments to consider someone else's feelings.
>
> I have never experienced loneliness. If I'm nervous or scared, my twin is always there to talk me through those feelings. I know that she will always have my back, although she is also brutally honest when she thinks I'm in the wrong – much more honest than most friends! When we were young, we even had a private twin language. Sometimes, we finish each other's sentences, and there have been occasions when we have had similar dreams. Our connection is definitely much deeper than anything I have experienced with anyone else, because we have such similar thoughts and respond to situations in the same way. As a twin, you know what real love is.

Any issues are caused by outsiders. We have spent our lives being compared. Despite being identical, many people try to find subtle differences and point them out – sometimes rather rudely. As a teenager, I broke my ankle and, as a result, put on weight because I couldn't play sport. This became a source of amusement to some family and friends because, for the first time, our faces and bodies didn't look the same. They didn't consider my feelings, as they pointed out my fatter face or tummy; it was as if I was an exhibit in a museum rather than a girl with fragile feelings. Sometimes, twins are made to feel like a freak of nature. Exam results were always difficult because I was more academic than my sister. I can remember having to reassure her that results weren't everything and hiding my joy when I did well.

Growing up made things harder, too. The big life decisions like where to go to university were challenging because we had to consider how easily we would cope with separation – how far would be simply too far? Having never spent a night away from her, suddenly we could be a five-hour plane ride apart. Meeting partners was complicated because a twin is the person closest to you threatening other relationships. My fiancé knew that unless my twin approved, he had no chance of marrying me. That's not an easy scenario, as you can imagine!

Task 3.1

According to Text 3.1, what are the advantages of being an identical twin and what problems can it cause?

1   How many strands does this task have? What are they?

   ....

   ....

   ....

2 Read Text 3.1 again and list all the main points, the details and the examples in Table 3.1.

Main point	Details	Examples

Table 3.1

3   Copy out your list of main points in a logical order in your notebook. Check that you have not repeated any ideas. If two points are similar, try to **synthesise** them into one point.

> **KEY TERM**
>
> **synthesise:** to combine or draw together similar points

3.2 Remodelling the text

4   Rewrite the following paragraph, reducing the number of words by replacing the following phrases (written in bold in the paragraph) with a new word or phrase. When you have finished, read the text aloud to check the words added read fluently with no awkwardness. Then make any corrections necessary.

opening and searching though every drawer and cupboard in his house

a time to see the eye specialist

go by bus or train

document showing the times of the departures

daughters and sons

The old man was looking for his glasses, but despite **opening and searching through every drawer and cupboard in his house**, he couldn't find them. He decided to visit the optician in the nearby town and rang to arrange **a time to see the eye specialist**. As he couldn't drive his car without his glasses, he would have to **go by bus or train**. However, without his glasses, he couldn't read the small print on the **document showing the times of the departures**. In the end, he decided to telephone his **daughters and sons** to see if one of them could take him.

....

....

....

....

....

....

....

LANGUAGE FOCUS: FORMALITY

The formality of a piece of writing refers to whether or not it follows certain standards and **conventions** of language and grammar. A definition of formal language is best given by a definition of what it is not. Signs of an informal piece of writing include **chatty language** and conversational tone, abbreviations or contractions. Informal pieces also use the **active voice** rather than the **passive voice** of the verb, as well as **direct speech**.

A formal piece of writing can therefore be characterised by:

- a more 'serious' tone and language
- a lack of contractions (for example, 'do not' instead of 'don't')
- the passive rather than the active voice (e.g. 'It could be viewed as . . .' rather than 'I view it as . . .')
- **reported speech** rather than direct speech
- no slang or colloquial expressions (e.g. 'The exhibit in the shop window was vibrant and eye-catching', not 'The shop window looked cool and funky'.)

KEY TERMS

conventions: the 'rules' of how a story is told or a piece of writing is set out

chatty language: the type of language and vocabulary you would use when talking to family or a close friend about unimportant things

active voice: where the subject of a sentence is the person or thing performing the action

passive voice: where the verb is placed before the person or thing, so the verb acts upon the subject

direct speech: the exact words a person says, marked by speech marks

reported speech: a speaker's words reported rather than stated directly, using changes of person and tense, and governed by a reporting verb (e.g. 'he **said**', 'she **stated**')

5 In your notebook, rewrite Text 3.2, using a more formal and neutral tone.

Text 3.2

The Burj Khalifa is an absolutely whopping skyscraper in Dubai. It measures an incredible 829.8 metres. Wow! Unamazingly, it's the tallest building in the whole wide world, and loads of people flock to the observation decks on floors 124 and 125. To get there in the lift takes less than 60 seconds, so it's a bit like being launched in a rocket and makes your tummy go funny. The views of Dubai from the top are mighty impressive though, especially when the sun is going down, although it gets really packed at that time too, so it's hard to get to the window. Everything below you looks like tiny toys, even some of the skyscrapers! I had to queue for ages to get to use one of the telescopes to zoom in on the famous landmarks in Dubai. It was brilliant being able to see things like Palm Jumeirah Island and the ocean, but also being able to see as far as the desert was mind-blowing! The outdoor terrace was a bit scary – I must admit I thought my hair was going to get blown off my head! Don't think that's a great place for people terrified of heights – they should stay safely behind the glass windows!

6   In your notebook, write planning notes for Task 3.2, a summary task.

> **Task 3.2**
>
> According to Text 3.3, why are young people less likely to learn to drive and own a car than previous generations? You should write no more than 120 words.

Text 3.3

> Have Millennials and Gen Z fallen out of love with the motor car? Evidence suggests that fewer young people are learning to drive than in previous generations, and many have no intention of ever owning a car at all. Recent innovations in goods and services have made online orders and home deliveries easier than ever before, so owning a car is less essential than in the past. Online taxi apps mean that travelling longer distances is easier, and of course, the cost of running a car has increased, leading many young people to believe that personal vehicles are a luxury they neither need nor can afford.
>
> In addition, there is evidence to suggest that some young people are anxious about the responsibilities of driving on increasingly busy roads, making them reluctant to take driving lessons. They are also more likely to be environmentally conscious – aware of the impact of mass car ownership on global warming. They are concerned about the increase in extreme weather conditions and want to play a part in adopting a greener lifestyle through recycling and cutting their carbon footprint.
>
> Developments in technology mean that it's possible to keep in touch with friends without leaving home. As a result, people don't need to go out to socialise as much as young people did in the past. They can just pull out their smartphones! However, this has led to isolation and fragile mental health in some young people, particularly after the Covid-19 pandemic.
>
> Young people tend to move to be where the jobs are, and that means living in cities where car ownership is unnecessary due to good public transportation. In cities, owning a car is a liability due to restricted parking, and sometimes there are charges for driving in congested areas. Many young people are paying university loans and high rents, so they can't find the spare cash to buy a car or the funds to pay for insurance, fuel and repairs. Cars devour cash that young folk simply don't have.
>
> Whether this trend will continue remains to be seen, but it certainly seems to be the case that the thrill of independence that the motor car once posed has lost its attraction.

7   Look again at your notes for Activity 6. Insert lines and arrows to show where you would link similar ideas and avoid repetition.

8   Use your notes to write your summary in your notebook.

9 Check your summary using this checklist.

Have you used a formal **register** – no chatty asides or informal expressions? ☐

Is the tone neutral – no opinions or comments? ☐

Have you used your own words – are there quotes, lifted sentences or phrases that could have been changed? ☐

Have you avoided repetition? ☐

Have you synthesised similar points? ☐

Have you organised the points helpfully? ☐

Is the summary an appropriate length – close to 120 words? ☐

> **KEY TERM**
>
> **register:** the level of formality in a piece of writing

3.3 Developing a coherent summary

> **LANGUAGE FOCUS: SENTENCE TYPES**
>
> To write fluently and coherently, it is important to use a range of sentence types. There are three main sentence types: simple, compound and complex. All three have an equally important role in writing fluently.
>
> - Simple sentences have only one main verb. For example, 'She wore the red coat.' Simple sentences are important when making a strong point, but using too many of them can make your writing feel disjointed and less interesting to read.
>
> - Compound sentences have more than one verb. When writing a compound sentence, you use **coordinating conjunctions** to combine two simple sentences. For example, 'She saw the darkening clouds gathering **so** she ran for shelter.' Compound sentences are useful for making connections between related ideas.
>
> - Complex sentences use **subordinate clauses** to add information. For example, 'Although she was scared,[1] she went into the dark house alone.' The subordinate clause does not make sense on its own or form a complete sentence like the main clause.

> **KEY TERMS**
>
> **coordinating conjunction:** a word such as 'and', 'but', 'or' that joins two words or two main clauses in a sentence
>
> **subordinate clause:** in grammar, a clause that cannot form a sentence alone but adds information to the main clause

[1] This is the subordinate clause.

10 Combine the following sentences using a coordinating conjunction or a subordinate clause. You may have to change the word order.

a The boys walked over five kilometres to school. Their bus had broken down.

....

....

b She lived in a very small village. She worked in a large town.

....

....

c The roads heading to the coast were exceptionally busy that morning. It was a public holiday.

....

....

d Muhammad was a diligent student. He enjoyed all his school subjects.

....

....

e Aisha loved listening to pop music in her bedroom. She played it using her smartphone and a wireless speaker.

....

....

f Jerry's car kept making a strange noise. The car needed a new engine.

....

....

g Tula drove down the road. She could see a traffic jam ahead of her and slowed down.

....

....

h Priya's father swept her up into his arms. He told her how wonderful it was to see her again.

....

....

i The herd of cows ambled along the track. They were almost at the milking sheds.

....

....

j The jet was speeding through the sky. It left a trail of vapour behind it.

....

....

11 Look at this plan of a summary task on the advantages and disadvantages of school uniforms. Use the plan to write the summary in your notebook.

> **Notes:**
> - encourages a community identity
> - stops inequality as everyone wears the same clothes
> - stops classroom becoming a fashion show
> - reduces bullying in school
> - no competition to be the 'coolest' dresser
> - it's obvious which school a student goes to
> - improves behaviour outside school
> - easy to identify a student's school if they misbehave
> - stops individuality by taking choice away
> - uniform is an added expense
> - sorting out uniform issues takes teachers' time up
> - some students wear inappropriate accessories anyway
> - some parents can't afford it
> - students start to wear it scruffily after a while

12 Look at the sample response to a summary question on the advantages and disadvantages of taking a holiday job. It is over 300 words long, so it needs to be shortened to about 120 words without losing any of the main points. Rewrite the summary in your notebook, making the following changes:

- Reword some parts of the summary to make it more concise.
- Remove any repeated points.
- Reorganise the summary by putting similar points together.

> Taking a temporary job in the holidays can have lots of advantages, as it allows a person to earn lots of extra money that they can spend on buying lots of extra items, including luxury items like holidays which they might not be able to afford usually. If you take a job in the holidays, it is usually the kind of work that doesn't need you to have that much experience so you can get a job quite easily because it doesn't matter if you haven't done that kind of work before. It can also be a good experience and help you in your future when you are applying for jobs in the future because it gives you something to put on your CV or resume which future employers may like. So, it could help you to develop skills to get a job in the future. Having a holiday job is also good for building up and developing useful skills like communicating with the public, solving problems, handling money, etc., etc. It allows you to show that you are reliable and honest.

> However, there are also lots of disadvantages to taking a job in the holidays. If you are a student, it may take up time when you should be studying, so you end up not getting enough work done and getting poor grades. This is a bad thing as you won't do so well. If you have a family, you won't see them in the holidays because you will be working the whole time which is another bad thing. You would also get really tired, and you also might get exhausted, too. Lots of holiday jobs make you work during the evenings and weekends too, because they make the temporary workers do all the shifts that are in antisocial hours because the main staff don't want them. But you would also get really good experience, so that may be something you don't mind. You will also earn extra money, too.

Practice questions

13 Read Text 3.4, then respond to questions 13a and 13b in your notebook.

    a   According to Text 3.4, what rules have been adopted for mobile phone use in this school and why is this the correct approach?

        Use continuous writing (not note form) and use your own words as far as possible.

        Your summary should not be more than 120 words.

        Up to 10 marks are available for reading and up to 5 marks for writing.   [15]

    b   Assess the writer's attitude towards developing responsibility and good manners in young people? Use **three** details from Text 3.4 to support your answer.   [5]

In Text 3.4, the deputy head of an international secondary school explains the unique approach his school has taken to the use of mobile phones.

Text 3.4

> While the reasons for an outright ban on mobile phones in some settings may be compelling, we have decided not to ban them outright but instead incorporate them into daily life, but with some clear parameters by which students are, and are not, allowed to use them.

The reasons we have done this are threefold. Firstly, our campus and educational systems are intrinsically connected with mobile phones. Phones serve as indispensable tools for accessing student timetables, facilitating communication and sharing crucial documents for lessons. As such, it is helpful for staff and students to have access to devices. Secondly, we maintain an open campus and consider it a matter of safety not to deprive our young learners of their phones. Thirdly, we want to teach students the art of self-regulation. Our objective is not to mould students who merely follow orders when they must, and then ignore them the moment they can.

Instead, we strive to nurture young individuals who are capable of making responsible choices and understand that while mobile phones have become an integral part of life, they should exercise restraint by knowing when to put the phone down and their head up.

To help make this message clear, we have developed a simple mantra: 'Meet, feet, eat.'

Meet

All gatherings, including assemblies and year-group meetings, are designated as technology-free zones. Any use of mobile phones in these areas results in confiscation. Furthermore, in class, students are required to place their phones in designated boxes on the front desk, unless explicitly permitted by the teacher for a specific task. During extracurricular activities, students are also expected to refrain from phone use and focus on the session they are taking part in.

Feet

We encourage students to walk with their heads held high and their eyes open, fostering a sense of awareness and presence, and engaging with those they meet. They should not be on their phones aimlessly scrolling while staring at their feet.

Eat

Our school maintains a strict policy against using technology in the school restaurant and during house meals. We believe in the importance of good manners, which means focusing on the company at the table.

Our approach is not one that blindly embraces all technology without acknowledging any potential negative consequences. It is aimed at preparing students for a future in which they will constantly encounter technological distractions but must learn to overcome this temptation.

Adapted from an article from www.tes.com

> Unit 4

Analysing and explaining writers' effects

> **LEARNING INTENTIONS**
>
> By the end of this unit, you will be able to:
>
> - understand how a writer's word choices convey meaning
> - explain the effects of writers' language choices
> - explore how words and phrases influence a reader
> - understand how writers use figurative language to create effects
> - analyse how and why writers use sensory language
> - apply strategies to help you explain how writers achieve effects and influence readers.

4.1 Understanding meanings and effects

1. Read Text 4.1. Work out the meanings of the words listed in Table 4.1 (in bold in Text 4.1), then use a dictionary to check whether you got them right.

Text 4.1

> He looked at the gushing water **tentatively**; he knew if he didn't make it to the opposite bank, he would be swept away and carried towards the dangerous rapids. His friends stood on the other side, **goading** him to jump onto the large rock **protruding** from the foaming swell in the middle of the river. He had to prove he was **worthy** of their friendship. His heart felt heavy as he considered his **puny** frame; he had never been a **proficient** athlete, particularly in the long jump, where his attempts were always **pathetic**. He shook his head and smiled **plaintively**.

4 Analysing and explaining writers' effects

Word	Meaning	Correct?
tentatively		
goading		
protruding		
worthy		
puny		
proficient		
pathetic		
plaintively		

Table 4.1

2   Choose six of the words from Activity 1 and write a sentence for each one.

   ....

   ....

   ....

   ....

   ....

   ....

3 Now look at this example of how different verb choices can change the meaning of a sentence:

Ali **smirked** as Amira walked into the room.

Ali **smiled** as Amira walked into the room.

Ali **beamed** as Amira walked into the room.

Explain how the words 'smirked', 'smiled' and 'beamed' (in bold) change the reader's impression of Ali's attitude in each sentence.

....

....

....

....

....

....

4 Choose the most appropriate verb from the list to complete each sentence.
Use each verb only once.

trickled   drizzled   pelted   poured   sprinkled   sprayed

- **a** It had .... all day leaving everything looking miserable and damp.
- **b** As the rain .... from the sky, the storm drains started to fill dangerously.
- **c** They ran down the street laughing as the freezing rain .... them.
- **d** She watched sadly as the rain .... down the outside of the window pane.
- **e** As the bus passed them, the rainwater .... over the windscreen distorting her vision.
- **f** She laughed as her brother .... her with the hose pipe as she ran across the lawn.

4.2 Language chosen for deliberate impact

> **LANGUAGE FOCUS: VERBS, ADJECTIVES AND ADVERBS**
>
> **Verbs**
>
> Dramatic verbs help the reader to understand how an action is performed more clearly. For example:
>
> - The father **rushed** to school to collect his daughter.
>
> The writer could have said, 'The father went to school to collect his daughter', but 'rushed' (in bold) indicates a sense of urgency and alerts the reader to the fact that something may be wrong. In this way, the writer has added meaning to the sentence.
>
> **Adjectives**
>
> Writers also add meaning through their choice of adjectives. Look at the extreme adjectives in this sentence:
>
> - The **ancient** tree towered above them as they gazed at its **huge** trunk in awe.
>
> The adjectives 'ancient' and 'huge' (in bold) make the tree sound far more impressive than 'old' or 'large' would have done.
>
> **Adverbs**
>
> Adverbs are also used to create deliberate effects. For example:
>
> - She smiled **cruelly** and shut the door.
>
> The adverb 'cruelly' (in bold) completely changes the sentence, indicating the character's unpleasantness and desire to cause pain.

5   Read Text 4.2. Decide whether each of the following words (also written in bold in Text 4.2) is a dramatic verb, an adverb or an adjective, then put each one in the correct column of Table 4.2.

| eerily | ominous | expansive | crept | stealthily | startling |
| flapping | ruffled | pounded | furiously | beat | |

Text 4.2

> The moon was **eerily** white in the dark night sky, creating **ominous** shadows across the **expansive** field. He held his breath as he **crept** forward **stealthily** along the hedgerow, making as little noise as possible. Suddenly, a **startling** screech filled the air, and **flapping** wings **ruffled** the edge of his face as a large bird took flight from the hedge. His heart **pounded furiously** as if trying to **beat** its way out of his chest.

Verb	Adverb	Adjective
	eerily	

Table 4.2

6   Read Text 4.2 aloud to gain a sense of the atmosphere. Describe the kind of atmosphere the writer has created.

....

....

....

....

4 Analysing and explaining writers' effects

7 Choose three examples of words or phrases from Text 4.2 that support your answer to Activity 6, and explain the meaning and effect of each choice.

....

....

....

....

....

....

....

8 Explain the **connotations** of the following words written in bold in sentences a–e:

miserly   weedy   gang   meticulous   neglected

a He had always been **miserly** when it came to birthdays and other family celebrations.

....

....

b He really wanted to be good at sport, but others always told him he was too **weedy**.

....

....

c She was upset when her brother wouldn't let her join his **gang**.

....

....

d He was **meticulous** when he planned a journey overseas.

....

....

> **KEY TERM**
>
> **connotations:** the ideas, feelings and associations that a particular word evokes in a reader, in addition to the main meaning of the word

37

e The house seemed **neglected** and cold.

....

....

9 Read Text 4.3, a news article. Make a list of the emotive words the writer uses.

....

....

....

Text 4.3

> **Bored youths riot in front of horrified shoppers!**
>
> A mob of disaffected youths ran riot in a shopping centre yesterday – because they were bored in the long school holiday.
>
> It happened when one thoughtless youngster posted an open invitation on social media, encouraging every 14-year-old in the city to invade the shopping centre at midday.
>
> Innocent shoppers at the centre (many with tiny toddlers) were terrified when swarms of schoolchildren amassed in the main concourse[1], playing brash music at top volume, screaming hysterically and chasing one another up and down the escalators.
>
> 'I was horrified!' said one shopper. 'It was like being in a war zone. I gathered up my children and escaped as quickly as I could.' Others fled into shops to escape from the brawl.
>
> Large numbers of police rushed to the complex after several frantic alerts by concerned members of the public. They were able to quickly calm the situation by switching off the music and asking the youths to leave. Later, some of the young people told us that they were bored at home because there was nothing to do, and they just met up to have some fun.

GLOSSARY

[1]**concourse:** large open inside area

10 Note down how the emotive language conveys the writer's attitude towards each of the following:

a the young people who gathered at the shopping centre

....

....

....

....

4 Analysing and explaining writers' effects

b the shoppers

....

....

....

....

11 Write a paragraph explaining how the emotive language in Text 4.3 affects the reader's response to the incident in the shopping centre.

....

....

....

....

....

....

....

4.3 Exploring figurative language

> **LANGUAGE FOCUS: FIGURATIVE LANGUAGE**
>
> You should already be familiar with the literary devices **simile** and **metaphor**, which are used to draw comparisons for effect, as well as **personification**.
>
> **Hyperbole**
> Hyperbole is where a writer deliberately exaggerates to add emphasis or make something more dramatic. For example:
>
> - That day seemed to last forever: she couldn't take her eyes off the clock and each minute passing felt like a day itself. The waiting was tortuous.
>
> The exaggerations used in 'last forever', 'felt like a day itself' and 'tortuous' convey the character's extreme frustration. They help the reader to understand the character's impatience and anticipation.
>
> **Onomatopoeia**
> Onomatopoeia is when a writer uses a word in which the sound imitates the thing being described. For example:
>
> - The jangling bells danced as the clanging sound rang out over the village.
>
> The sounds created by 'jangling', 'clanging' and 'rang' evoke the sounds and movements of the bells. This appeals to the reader's sense of hearing and brings the action to life. Reading a text aloud can help you to spot onomatopoeia and to explain why it is effective as a literary device.
>
> **Alliteration**
> Alliteration is the repetition of a sound or letter at the beginning of words. Writers use it to create a rhythm or to create a particular atmosphere. For example:
>
> - The raging river roared over the boulders and rocks.
>
> Here, the alliterative use of the letter 'r' creates a sense of speed and aggression that accentuates the wild nature of the water.

> **KEY TERMS**
>
> **simile:** a type of figurative language in which one thing is compared to something else using the words 'as' or 'like'
>
> **metaphor:** a type of comparison that describes one thing as if it were something else
>
> **personification:** a type of figurative language in which an object is described as if it has human characteristics

12 Draw lines to match each sentence with the correct literary device.

a	If I live for a million years, I will never understand the point of algebra.
b	The sand was swirling upwards like a series of mini tornadoes.
c	She loved the sound of her boots crunching through the autumn leaves.
d	The raindrops danced joyfully across the street in the moonlight.
e	The sea swirled stormily, trying to devour everything in its reach.
f	His heart was a block of ice that couldn't be thawed.

1	alliteration
2	simile
3	onomatopoeia
4	personification
5	metaphor
6	hyperbole

4 Analysing and explaining writers' effects

13 For each of these literary devices, write a sentence to describe a long journey by train.

a Simile

....

....

b Metaphor

....

....

c Alliteration

....

....

d Personification

....

....

e Hyperbole

....

....

f Onomatopoeia

....

....

14 Read Text 4.4, which describes a kayaking trip in New Zealand. Highlight examples of **figurative language** and **sensory images** that the writer has used. You may want to read Text 4.4 aloud to help spot the sensory language used.

Text 4.4

> The wind had eased, but it was still raining when we reached Deep Cove. A nearby waterfall beat its steady, ominous thunder, sheets of spray spurting like high-pressure steam where the cascade struck the surface of the fiord.[1] I traced the gushing plume of water upwards for 500 m. Looking west, sea, mountain and cloud merged into an ethereal[2] landscape, like a watercolour painting that had a life of its own, constantly evolving at the whim of rain, light and wind.
>
> Elsewhere, bare granite gleamed like slivers of bone through the verdant[3] flesh of the forest. These great scars, Ben told us, were created by 'tree avalanches' where the thin layer of rich humus[4] covering the cliff faces suddenly gave way, sending huge swathes of forest crashing into the fiord.
>
> Adapted from 'Wet, Wet, Wet' by William Gray

KEY TERMS

figurative language: words and phrases used not with their basic meaning but with a more imaginative meaning to create a special effect; figurative language techniques include simile, metaphor and personification

sensory image: an image that appeals to the reader's senses: sight, sound, touch, taste and smell

GLOSSARY

[1]**fiord:** a long, narrow body of water

[2]**ethereal:** not of this world

[3]**verdant:** green

[4]**humus:** soil

15 Look at this sample answer, which explores the effect of the figurative language in Text 4.4 by focusing on the sensory images.

> *The metaphorical description 'beat its steady, ominous thunder' suggests that the sound of the waterfall is deafening and also rhythmic. The writer captures the impressiveness of it by using the word 'ominous', as the sound is so loud that it fills him with a feeling of dread and awe.*

Choose five other examples of figurative language and explain why they are used effectively in the text. Make sure at least two of your examples focus on sensory language. Use the sample answer to help you structure your answers.

a ....

....

....

....

b ....

....

....

c ....
....
....
....

d ....
....
....

e ....
....
....

4.4 Explaining how writers achieve effects and influence readers

Read Text 4.5, then complete Activities 16–18.

Text 4.5

"We're off now."

"They'll never catch us."

"We'll never go back till we're rich."

The three of them sat on the hilltop and looked down at the town, a dark reeking[1] pit, where the first lights were glowing like embers in a raked-out campfire. They had already come over a mile. And on the other side of the hill lay . . .

Well, Brian knew. With his thin legs like a linnet[2] and his great brain behind spectacles like oyster shells, he had it all worked out. He knew just what roots and leaves you could eat and which would stretch you out like a cod on a slab.[3] He knew the constellations[4] and so could tell which direction to travel in at night. He said he knew how to make a fire by rubbing sticks together and what sort of wood these sticks had to be. He had read how to make a canoe out of a log, by burning it hollow with little fires. The other two, Bert and Bloodnut, trusted him completely.

"When shall we eat?" asked Bert. "We've got to keep our strength up."

He had cheese and a tin of tongue. Bloodnut had a packet of dates and a banana. Brian had nothing.

"Eat?" demanded Brian indignantly. "Eat? Tonight we've got to keep going. They'll be out after us by eleven. We want to be far away by morning. Safe. Then we can eat. Then we'll hunt something."

Bloodnut fingered the shilling[5] in his back pocket. He was already wishing he had bought a meat pie.

"Come on." Brian got up. The other two got up. Brian looked up at the sky but there were no stars yet. He led off in the direction away from the town.

From 'The Other Side of the Hill' by Ted Hughes

GLOSSARY

[1]**reeking:** having a strong, unpleasant smell

[2]**linnet:** a small bird

[3]**slab:** a thick, flat piece of stone or wood

[4]**constellation:** a group of stars that seem to have formed a pattern and which have been given a name

[5]**shilling:** an old British coin

16 To practise zooming out, write a short paragraph explaining what is happening in this extract.

....

....

....

....

....

4 Analysing and explaining writers' effects

17 To practise zooming in, answer the following questions, looking more closely at the character descriptions.

  a Look at the physical description of Brian in the sentence beginning 'With his thin . . . oyster shells' (lines 8–9). What impression does this give the reader of Brian and why?

  ....

  ....

  ....

  b How does the writer develop Brian's character in the same paragraph?

  ....

  ....

  ....

  ....

  ....

  ....

  c Identify a phrase in the paragraph which suggests that Brian may not be telling the truth. How does that make the final sentence of the paragraph – 'The other two . . . trusted him completely' – humorous for the reader?

  ....

  ....

  ....

  ....

  d What impression is created by the sentence 'Brian looked up at the sky but there were no stars yet' in the final paragraph?

  ....

  ....

  ....

  ....

18 Using the 'onion' strategy, complete Table 4.3 to explain the effects of six interesting phrases from Text 4.5 on the reader. Three have been chosen for you; select three more of your own.

Choice of language / literary technique	Example / quote	Effect
Direct speech	'We'll never go back till we're rich.'	
Metaphor	'a dark reeking pit'	
Simile	'like embers in a raked-out campfire'	

Table 4.3

4 Analysing and explaining writers' effects

Practice questions

Now read Text 4.6, which describes the arrival of the monsoon rains after a period of drought. Then complete Activities 19–21.

Text 4.6

One day, as Kulfi was at the bedroom window looking at the street, prepared to sit through another seemingly endless stretch of time until Ammaji finally cooked and served her dinner, all of a sudden a shadow fell across the sun and magically, as quickly as a winter's day tumbles into smoky evening and then night, the white-lit afternoon deepened into the colour of old parchment[1] as the sky darkened. Curtains billowed white out of every window. Bits of newspaper and old plastic bags turned cartwheels in the indigo[2] streets. The air thinned and stirred in a breeze that brought goose bumps out upon her arms. 'Look!' Kulfi shouted. 'Here comes the rain!'

She could hear the sound of cheering from the bazaar.[3] And she watched the children in the street leap like frogs, unable to keep still in their excitement. 'It's getting cold,' they shouted, and pretended to shake. 'It's going to rain.' They wrestled and tussled with each other in an exuberance of spirit, while the grown-ups hurried, in this shifting, shadowed light to get to the market and back, to bring in the washing, to carry in string cots. They raised their hands in greeting to each other. 'At last! The monsoon!'… The rain had come to Shahkot. The monsoon[4] was in town. Kulfi watched with unbelievable elation as the approaching smell of rain spiked the air like a flower, as the clouds shifted in from the east, reached the trees at the town's edge and moved in.

from 'Hullabaloo in the Guava Orchard' by Kiran Desai

GLOSSARY

[1]**parchment:** ancient paper

[2]**indigo:** deep violet-blue

[3]**bazaar:** market

[4]**monsoon:** rainy season

CAMBRIDGE IGCSE™ FIRST LANGUAGE ENGLISH: WORKBOOK

19 Use your own words to explain what the writer suggests about Kulfi's life in the phrase 'another seemingly endless stretch of time' (line 2).

....

....

....

....

.... [3]

20 Use **one** example from the following extract from Text 4.6 to explain how the writer uses language to describe what Kulfi sees outside as the rain arrives. **Use your own words in your explanation.**

'. . . all of a sudden a shadow fell across the sun and magically, as quickly as a winter's day tumbles into smoky evening and then night, the white-lit afternoon deepened into the colour of old parchment as the sky darkened. Curtains billowed white out of every window. Bits of newspaper and old plastic bags turned cartwheels in the indigo streets. The air thinned and stirred in a breeze that brought goose bumps out upon her arms.'

....

....

....

....

....

.... [5]

21 Re-read paragraph 2. Choose **three** powerful words or phrases from paragraph 2 to analyse how the writer uses language to describe people's reactions to the monsoon rains.

Write about 200 to 250 words.

Up to 10 marks are available for the content of your answer.

....

....

....

....

48

[10]

> Unit 5

Extended response to reading

LEARNING INTENTIONS

By the end of this unit, you will be able to:

- select, evaluate and use relevant ideas and details from a text to create a new piece of writing
- develop ideas from a text using inference
- understand the features of articles, speeches, journals, letters, interviews and reports
- write for different audiences and purposes using appropriate language
- create a convincing voice using a range of vocabulary and sentence structures.

5.1 Conventions of text types

1 Look at Texts 5.1 and 5.2. Which of the following text types is each one? Note down the features you identified to provide evidence for your answer.

speech   letter   article   journal   interview   report

Text 5.1

> **To: The Town Planning Committee**
> **From: The Residents' Association of Blocks 54–100**
> Outcome of the residents' emergency meeting
>
> On Tuesday 12 February, the Residents' Association met to discuss the possible destruction of the recreational area to build more housing blocks. Several observations about the planning application were made. Firstly, some residents pointed out that with the loss of this land, there would be nowhere local for parents to take their children to play, as the nearest public park is over 3 km away. This would leave those without access to a car unable to reach an area where children can run and play.
>
> Another great loss for the community concerns the older population who use the recreation area to meet and socialise. Without this area, many older people would have nowhere outside to go, depriving them of sunlight and the health benefits it brings, particularly in the winter months.

Text type:

....

Purpose and audience:

....

....

Register and tone:

....

....

Features identified:

....

....

Other features of this text type:

....

....

Text 5.2

Traffic-calming system causes chaos

It's gridlock out there!

A traffic-calming system designed to slow vehicles down near residential developments has created gridlock, according to drivers who regularly travel through New Town on their way to work, or to take children to school. One furious motorist said, 'It took me two hours to drop the kids off at school. I ended up late for work!' Other motorists spoke of being stationary in their cars for over 20 minutes. 'Whoever designed this needs to go back to school!' one motorist declared.

However, residents in the area argue that the number of accidents caused by speeding in recent years means that the council had to do something to increase safety for them.

Possible solutions

When we spoke to council representatives, they explained it will take some time for motorists and pedestrians to get used to the new layout.
'At the moment, motorists don't follow the new regulations, leading to confusion,' their spokesperson said. The council plans to improve the signage.

Text type:

....

Purpose and audience:

....

....

Register and tone:

....

....

Features identified:

....

....

Other features of this text type:

....

....

2   Fill in Table 5.1 to identify the features of the four other text types from the list.

Text type:	Text type:
Main features:	Main features:
Text type:	**Text type:**
Main features:	Main features:

Table 5.1

5.2 Evaluating and using ideas from a text

Read Text 5.3, which is part of a longer narrative. Raka, who lives in a large city, has had a serious illness. She has been sent to stay with her great-grandmother, Nanda Kaul, in her country house in India to help her recovery. It is the first time they have met.

Text 5.3

Nanda Kaul [was] standing under the apricot trees with her hands pressed together before her and watching the child come in through the gate where the pine trees stood bending and twisting extravagantly in the wind as though miming welcome in a modern ballet.

Raka meant the moon, but this child was not round-faced, calm or radiant. As she shuffled up the garden path with a sling bag weighing down one thin, sloping shoulder and her feet in old sandals heavy with dust, Nanda Kaul thought she looked like one of those dark crickets that leap up in fright but do not sing, or a mosquito, minute and fine, on thin, precarious legs.

But 'Raka' she nevertheless said, hoping somehow to relate the name to the child and wondering if she would ever get used to seeing this child in her garden.

Raka slowed down, dragged her foot, then came towards her great-grandmother with something despairing in her attitude, saying nothing. She sucked at the loose, curly elastic of an old, broken straw hat that drooped over her closely cropped head like a straw bag. She turned a pair of extravagantly large and somewhat bulging eyes about in a way that made the old lady feel more than ever her resemblance to an insect…

Turning slightly, [Raka] saw a scraggy-necked hen pecking beneath a bush of blue hydrangeas at some pieces of broken china.

Then she raised her small, shorn head on its very thin and delicate neck and regarded the apricot trees, the veranda [and the house]. She listened to the wind in the pines and the cicadas all shrilling incessantly in the sun with her unfortunately large and protruding ears, and thought she had never before heard the sound of silence.

Then it was not possible to postpone the meeting any longer and both moved a step closer to one another and embraced because they felt they must. There was a sound of bones colliding. Each felt how bony, angular and unaccommodating the other was and they quickly separated.

'Child, how ill you have been!' Nanda Kaul exclaimed involuntarily, leaving her hand for a moment on the straight hard shield of the thin shoulder. 'How ill. How thin it's made you.'

> Raka pulled at the slack elastic with some embarrassment and rolled her eyes around to follow the flight of the hoopoe bird that suddenly darted out of the tree. She saw the old lady who murmured at her as another pine tree, the grey sari, a rock – all components of the bareness and stillness of the garden.
>
> To Nanda Kaul she was still an intruder, an outsider, a mosquito flown up from the plains to tease and worry. With a blatant lack of warmth, she sighed, 'Well, better come in,' and she led her across the wavy tiles of the veranda to her room.
>
> from 'Fire on the Mountain' by Anita Desai

In Text 5.3, there are two characters, so you could be asked to write a new text from either of those characters' **perspectives**. This means creating and developing a convincing **voice** as well as modifying the ideas in the text to view it through their eyes. Read Task 5.1 below, then complete Activities 3, 4 and 5 which will help you to plan your response.

KEY TERMS

perspective: the 'angle' that a story or account is told from – whose 'eyes' the reader sees it through

voice: the personality and attitude of the narrator

Task 5.1

You are Raka. Write a letter to your mother to let her know you have arrived safely at your great-grandmother's house.

In your letter, include your thoughts and feelings about:

- your great-grandmother and the way she acted when you arrived
- the house, garden and its location
- whether you think your time there will help you get better.

LANGUAGE FOCUS: WORD SELECTION

Word selection is a key aspect of conveying voice and situation. The words you choose give a sense of a narrator's personality and help to bring situations to life for your reader. Consider this example from the sample response in Activity 3:

- 'Her expression was weird: she looked repulsed, like I was a horrible bug or something.'

This example is based on this section of text: 'She turned a pair of extravagantly large and somewhat bulging eyes about in a way that made the old lady feel more than ever her resemblance to an insect.'

Here, the language used reflects the fact that Raka is a child in an unfamiliar situation dealing with something difficult; for example, 'weird', 'horrible bug' and the 'or something' adds a sense of uncertainty or lack of confidence.

It is clear that she has sensed her great-grandmother's discomfort about her being there and is equally unsettled. The response has changed the perspective and captured Raka's feelings.

Notice that suitable word choices not only convey voice and personality, but they also demonstrate your skills as a writer.

3   Look at the first paragraph of a student's response to the first bullet point in the sample question, then plan the next two paragraphs using Table 5.2. Look for ideas in Text 5.3 as to how you could adapt the text to create a convincing voice. Remember that the third bullet point of a task often requires more inference from using clues in the text to develop the answer.

> Dear Mother,
>
> I arrived at Great-grandmother's today after a long journey. She wasn't pleased to see me and didn't welcome me at the gate. She just stood there watching which made me feel self-conscious. My bag was heavy, and I could hear my sandals shuffling – I told you they were too big for me – and they were covered with dust so I felt embarrassed. She was staring at me constantly, and I don't think she liked me. Her expression was weird: she looked repulsed, like I was a horrible bug or something. She said my name 'Raka' weirdly, as though she was saying it for the first time. I didn't know what to do, so I began sucking on my hat elastic like an idiot. I'm sure she's cross about me coming and wants to be alone. I ended up staring awkwardly. Why did you send me here to stay with a strange old lady? She hugged me, but I could tell she didn't really want to. It took ages before she finally showed me to my room.

Bullet point	Ideas	Development / details
The house, garden and its location		
Whether you think your time there will help you get better		

Table 5.2

4   Write the two paragraphs you have planned in your notebook.

> **Task 5.2**
>
> You are Nanda Kaul. Write a journal entry for the night that Raka arrived. In your journal, reflect on:
>
> - your first impressions of the child
> - your concerns about having her to stay with you
> - how you behaved when she arrived.

5   Look at Task 5.2 which is also based on Text 5.3. Plan your answer to Task 5.2 by creating a table like Table 5.2 in your notebook to develop your ideas for each bullet point. Consider how you can develop your ideas through:

- creating a convincing voice for Nanda Kaul
- using ideas from the text to develop Nanda Kaul's feelings about having Raka to stay with her, as well as developing them to consider how she may reflect on her own behaviour
- adding details from the text to support them.

5.3 Developing ideas

Read Text 5.4, in which a travel journalist goes on a trip to spot snow leopards in a remote mountain village in the Indian Himalayas. Then complete Activities 6 and 7.

Text 5.4

"Shan![1] Shan!" The call comes at breakfast amid a sharp clatter of cutlery. I hurl my fork towards the table, scrambled eggs flying, and bolt for the door.

Outside, snow-bloated clouds mottle the sky, the air is knife-cold – chill enough to make your joints ache – and I raise my binoculars with shaking hands. Two creatures are picking their way across the mountainside. My shoulders drop slightly – it's wolves. They trot nimbly past some fluttering flags, their bellies swollen from a recent feast.

It's an incredible sighting, but wolves are not why I am here. They are not why I've travelled to India's farthest reaches, through towns and mountains, to the remote foothills of the mighty Himalayas.

Because this is the land of the snow leopard. The tiny village of Ulley in West Ladakh is surrounded by mountains whose crags shelter these magnificent big cats. Here, a small clutch of houses teeters at a breathtaking 14,000 feet.

GLOSSARY

[1]**Shan:** the Bhoti word for snow leopard

Temperatures can plummet to minus 30° in winter and the air is thin and flighty, getting away from you when your lungs need it most. I'm holed up at The Snow Leopard Lodge, a homestay run by Tchewang Norbu, a local man with an almost superhuman ability to seek out the rare animals. The lodge is a vital means of employment for locals and keen-eyed villagers work as "spotters", scouring the ice-ravaged landscape for a flash of fur or the coil of a heavy tail.

Snow leopards have a colossal range, covering almost two million square kilometres in Central Asia. With only an estimated 6,500 left in the wild, unsurprisingly, seeing them is a struggle. "Needle in a haystack" doesn't cover it. These are hostile mountains with nooks and crannies, towering granite boulders and unreachable valleys. But take a walk and you'll know that "Shan" is watching you. You'll feel it in your blood. You may even see signs: scratch marks or pug marks in the dirt.

And so we spend our days getting "watched" by the snow leopards. We peer through our [tele]scopes, scour every rocky inch until our eyes ache and hike sweeping, snow-dusted valleys. We see golden eagles. We spot impressive mountain goats silhouetted against the sky. But we see no leopards.

The final morning dawns with the scent of mountain lavender in the air. We head out for a short hike, feverishly raking in the mountains for any signs of life. No joy. Back at the lodge, some of the group rest in their rooms, but I walk up to the spotters' point to scan with them for a while.

Up here, the landscape is as still as a stopped clock. Then spotter Namgyal begins to shout, "Shan! Shan! Shan!" His eyes are urgent, his words sitting in the air like smoke. Norbu rushes over, checks the scope, and turns to me, laughter lines etched into his face. My heart gallops. I put my eye to the glass. It's there all right. On the far ridge. Silhouetted like a sphinx – the unmistakable shape of a snow leopard. I shriek. The leopard hauls itself to its feet, tail as fat as a python that's just eaten. Suddenly, something else totters into view. The breath snags in my throat. It's a cub. No, two cubs. I blink cartoonishly as they clamber onto their mother's back, leaping from rock to rock. There are no guarantees in these mountains but to witness these creatures, hardy animals that are the embodiment of what is wild and unreachable, is to really feel like you've seen a ghost.

Adapted from 'Trailing the Snow Leopard in Mountainous Ladakh' by Lizzie Pook

6 Plan your answer to the following question:

You are Norbu, the owner of Snow Leopard Lodge. You are interviewed for a television travel show documenting the most unusual and interesting places in the world.

The interviewer asks you three questions:

- What is extraordinary about the landscape you live in and what are the challenges for visitors?
- What factors make it so difficult to spot a snow leopard?
- Why are people so fascinated by snow leopards and how do they react when they see one?

Remember that when writing an interview, your characters will be speaking aloud so adapt your language accordingly.

Your plan should cover:

- the voice you will write in – creating a convincing voice for Norbu
- the text type, audience and purpose
- the three bullet points in the task – the focus of each one, what ideas you need to look for and any other useful information
- changing the perspective from being a tourist to being local and the owner of the lodge where tourists stay adding details such as facts and figures to support the ideas.

Practice question

7 You are Norbu, the owner of Snow Leopard Lodge. You are interviewed for a television travel show documenting the most unusual and interesting places in the world.

The interviewer asks you three questions:

- What is extraordinary about the landscape you live in and what are the challenges for visitors?
- What factors make it so difficult to spot a snow leopard?
- Why are people so fascinated by snow leopards and how do they react when they see one?

Base your responses on what you have read in Text 5.4, but be careful to use your own words. Address each of the three bullet points.

Write about 250 to 300 words.

Up to 10 marks are available for reading and up to 10 marks for writing. [20]

> Unit 6

Reading practice

Use the skills and knowledge you have learnt in Units 1–5 to practice your reading skills.

Comprehension

Read **Text A: Junk food and health**, then answer **Questions 1a–1f**.

> **Text A: Junk food and health**
>
> Junk foods are often high in calories but lack nutrients and contain large quantities of salts, sugars or fats. They are also ultra-processed foods containing additives, preservatives and artificial colours – in other words, chemicals! The term 'junk' indicates that such foods offer little nutritional value and do not contribute to a healthy balanced diet. However, because they are easily accessible and affordable, they are popular.
>
> Junk foods are appealing, especially to children and teenagers who are attracted to the appearance, flavour and convenience of foods such as burgers, fries, pizzas, cakes, chocolate and sweets. Junk foods often dominate the diets of young adults who don't have time to prepare and cook fresh foods, relying instead on ready-made meals or take-out food to fit in with their busy schedules. Fresh foods such as meat, fish, vegetables, fruit and nuts are also more expensive than junk food, making junk food a tempting option for those on low incomes.
>
> The effect on young people's health is worrying. As junk food is high in calories and low in nutrients, eating it regularly can lead to higher levels of obesity and diabetes. There is also overwhelming evidence to suggest that anxiety and depression are linked to an unhealthy diet and inactivity.
>
> Moreover, junk food is addictive: consuming it releases a brain chemical called dopamine, creating a pleasurable feeling, and regular consumption leads to physical cravings, making it more difficult to ditch. Also, the junk food industry spends billions of dollars on marketing, so we are bombarded on a daily basis with targeted adverts enticing us to submit to the cravings.

Previously, this was a problem largely confined to Western countries. However, according to the World Health Organization (WHO), in the last decade, the junk food craze has spread to most of the globe, and obesity rates in young people have increased by more than 10%. The problem is spreading. WHO believes that governments worldwide need to restrict junk food marketing aimed at young people and children, increase education on healthy diets through schools and public health campaigns, and make fresh food cheaper.

There is no doubt that unless governments stop the bombardment of adverts enticing people to indulge in sugary, fatty foods by the powerful, unscrupulous and poorly regulated fast food industry, global health will decline rapidly.

Question 1

a   Give **two** examples of the types of chemicals used in junk foods, according to paragraph 1.

    .... [1]

b   Using your own words, explain what Text A means by:

    i   'large quantities' (line 2)

        ....

        .... [2]

    ii 'easily accessible' (line 7)

        ....

        .... [2]

c   Re-read paragraph 2 ('Junk foods are appealing . . . low incomes.').

    Give **two** reasons for young adults relying on junk foods.

    •   ....

    •   .... [2]

d Re-read paragraph 3 ('The effect . . . and inactivity.').

Identify **two** ways in which junk food has a negative impact on the health of young people – one physical and one mental.

Physical impact: ....

Mental impact: .... **[2]**

e Re-read paragraphs 4 and 5 ('Moreover, junk food is . . . cheaper.').

  i Explain why people may find it difficult to switch from a diet high in junk food to a healthier diet.

  ....

  ....

  .... **[3]**

  ii Using your own words, explain what the World Health Organization believes to be the reasons that the problem of eating junk food is getting worse rather than better.

  ....

  ....

  .... **[3]**

f Re-read paragraph 6 ('There is no doubt . . . decline rapidly.').

  i Why does the writer use the word 'bombardment' (line 37) rather than the word 'number' to describe the use of food adverts?

  ....

  .... **[2]**

  ii Explain what the writer suggests about the effect of fast food advertising in the phrase: 'enticing people to indulge in sugary, fatty foods' (line 38).

  ....

  ....

  ....

  .... **[3]**

  [Total: 20]

Summary task

Read **Text B**, about the growing popularity of following a vegan diet, and then answer **Questions 2a** and **2b**.

> **Text B: Is veganism really healthy?**
>
> Recently, adopting a vegan diet has been heralded as the best possible move for our health, leading to an explosion in the numbers of people eating a plant-based diet. One of veganism's biggest selling points is cutting out meat products, which have been shown to have a huge environmental impact and have been linked to serious diseases such as cancer as well as higher risks of heart attacks and strokes. Many vegans object to industrial-scale farming, which compromises animal welfare, and argue that the greenhouse gases released by farming contribute to climate change. Vegans tend to ingest fewer calories and eat more fruit and vegetables, leading to much lower risks of obesity and diabetes. As a result, far fewer people are likely to end up with related disabilities.
>
> However, a growing body of evidence is starting to suggest that a vegan diet may not be healthy after all. Studies have shown that vegans are more likely to suffer from anaemia due to a lack of iron in the diet, and their bones may break more easily due to calcium deficiency. This is because a diet excluding meat and dairy products misses key nutrients that are difficult to replace with plant-based foods. For example, the human body needs about 1300 milligrams of calcium a day to maintain healthy bones, which most people get from milk, cheese and yoghurts. A vegan would need to get their calcium from other foods, such as broccoli, spinach and rye bread. However, as there is far less calcium in these foods, they would have to eat huge and unmanageable amounts of them to absorb enough of the mineral on a daily basis.
>
> The range of vegan foods available has grown exponentially to match the increasing numbers of consumers purchasing them. Substitutes are offered for typical favourites such as bacon, burgers, sausages, cheese and even ice cream. The manufacturers claim they taste like the real thing, but that's rarely true. In addition, experts say that these foods are just as unhealthy as the non-vegan options – sometimes even worse! This is because to achieve the impossible task of getting tofu (or another yucky substitute) to look, feel and taste like meat or cheese, manufacturers have to use excessive quantities of fats, starch, sugars and salts, (ironically) making them higher in calories and lower in nutrients than the real foods.
>
> There is limited research available on the long-term effects of a plant-based diet, but a study of 26,000 females in middle age found that vegetarians (so still consuming dairy products) had a 33% higher risk of bone fractures, suggesting that female vegans have an even bigger risk of poor health. Although they may argue that it is possible to take supplements to mitigate the risks, there is evidence to suggest that not all supplements are absorbed effectively. Other studies indicate that, in the long term, a vegan diet can even cause hair loss as a result of deficiencies in iron or vitamin B12.

Question 2

a According to Text B, what are the advantages and disadvantages of a vegan diet?

Use continuous writing (not note form) and use your own words as far as possible.

Your summary should not be more than 120 words.

Up to 10 marks are available for reading and up to 5 marks for writing.

....

....

....

....

.... [15]

b What is the writer's attitude towards following a vegan diet? Use **three** details from Text B to support your answer.

....

....

....

....

.... [5]

[Total: 20]

Writers' meanings and effects

Read **Text C**, *My Life in France*, and then answer **Questions 3a–d**.

The writer is Julia Child, who became a famous television chef in America in the 1960s. In this extract from her memoir, she describes her first French meal when she and her husband moved to France after they married in 1948.

> **Text C: My life in France**
>
> At twelve-thirty we Flashed into Rouen. We passed the city's ancient and beautiful clock tower, and then its famous cathedral, magnificent with its stained-glass windows. The Michelin Guide directed us to Restaurant La Couronne (The Crown) – which had been built in 1345 in a medieval timbered house. Paul strode ahead, full of anticipation, but I hung back, concerned that I didn't look chic enough, that I wouldn't be able to communicate, and that the waiters would look down their noses at us American tourists.
>
> 5

It was warm inside, and the dining room was a comfortably old-fashioned brown-and-white space, neither humble or luxurious. At the far end was an enormous fireplace with a rotary spit, on which something was cooking that sent out heavenly aromas. We were greeted by the maître d'hôtel,[1] a slim middle-aged man with dark hair who carried himself with an air of gentle seriousness. Paul spoke to him, and the maître d' smiled and said something back in a familiar way, as if they were old friends. Then he led us to a nice table not far from the fireplace. The other customers were all French, and I noticed that they were treated with exactly the same courtesy as we were. Nobody rolled their eyes at us. Actually the staff seemed happy to see us [. . .]

Suddenly the dining room was filled with wonderfully intermixing aromas that I sort of recognised but couldn't name. The first smell was something oniony – "shallots," Paul identified it, "being sautéed in fresh butter." ("What's a shallot?" I asked, sheepishly. "You'll see," he said.) Then came a warm fragrance from the kitchen, which was probably a delicious sauce being reduced on the stove. This was followed by a whiff of something astringent: the salad being tossed in a big ceramic bowl with lemon, vinegar, olive oil, and a few shakes of salt and pepper.

My stomach gurgled with hunger.

I couldn't help noticing that the waiters carried themselves with a quiet joy as if their mission in life was to make their customers feel comfortable and well tended. One of them glided up to my elbow. Glancing at the menu, Paul asked him questions in rapid-fire French. The waiter seemed to enjoy the back and forth with my husband. Oh, how I itched to be in on their conversation! Instead I smiled and nodded uncomprehendingly, although I tried to absorb all that was going on around me.

We began our lunch with a half-dozen oysters which had a sensational briny flavour and a smooth texture that was entirely new and surprising. The oysters were served with rounds of a pale rye bread with a spread of unsalted butter. Paul explained that the French have special regions that produce individually flavoured butters [. . .]

Rouen is famous for its duck dishes, but after consulting the waiter Paul had decided to order sole meunière. It arrived whole: a large, flat Dover sole[2] that was perfectly browned in a sputtering butter sauce with a sprinkling of chopped parsley on top. The waiter carefully placed the platter in front of us and stepped back. I closed my eyes and inhaled the rising perfume. Then I lifted a forkful of fish to my mouth, took a bite and chewed slowly. The flesh of the sole was delicate with a light but distinct taste of the ocean that blended marvellously with the browned butter. I chewed slowly and swallowed. It was a morsel of perfection [. . .]

> **GLOSSARY**
>
> [1]**maître d'hôtel:** the person in charge of a restaurant or of the people who bring food to your table in a restaurant
>
> [2]**Dover sole:** a type of flat fish common in Europe

> Then came the salad laced with a slightly acidic vinaigrette. And I tasted my first real baguette – a crisp brown crust giving way to a slightly chewy, rather loosely textured pale-yellow interior, with a faint reminder of wheat and yeast in the taste. Yum! We followed our meal with a leisurely fromage blanc³ and ended with a strong dark filtered coffee [. . .]
>
> Paul and I floated out of the door into the brilliant sunshine and cool air. Our first lunch together in France had been absolute perfection. It was the most exciting meal of my life.
>
> From 'My Life in France' by Julia Child and Alex Prud'homme

GLOSSARY

³**fromage blanc:** a very soft cheese, similar to yogurt in taste and texture

Question 3

a   Identify a word or phrase from Text C which suggests the same idea as the phrases 'whole ambition' and 'slight hint' (in bold).

   i   The waiters' **whole ambition** was to please their customers and serve them well.

   .... [1]

   ii The flavour of the bread stirred a **slight hint** of the ingredients in her mind.

   .... [1]

b   Using your own words, explain what the writer means by the words 'aromas', 'identified', 'sheepishly' (in bold) in the extract from Text C.

   Suddenly the dining room was filled with wonderfully intermixing **aromas** that I sort of recognised but couldn't name. The first smell was something oniony – "shallots," Paul **identified** it, "being sautéed in fresh butter." ("What's a shallot?" I asked, **sheepishly**. "You'll see," he said.)

   i   aromas

   .... [1]

   ii   identified

   .... [1]

   iii sheepishly

   .... [1]

c Use **one** example from the following extract taken from Text C to explain how the writer uses language to suggest her impressions of the waiting staff.

Use your own words in your explanation.

'I couldn't help noticing that the waiters carried themselves with a quiet joy as if their mission in life was to make their customers feel comfortable and well tended. One of them glided up to my elbow. Glancing at the menu, Paul asked him questions in rapid-fire French. The waiter seemed to enjoy the back and forth with my husband. Oh, how I itched to be in on their conversation! Instead I smiled and nodded uncomprehendingly, although I tried to absorb all that was going on around me.'

....

....

....

....

....

.... [5]

d Choose **three** powerful words or phrases from the following extract from Text C to analyse how the writer uses language to describe her reaction to the food served.

'Rouen is famous for its duck dishes, but after consulting the waiter Paul had decided to order sole meunière. It arrived whole: a large, flat Dover sole that was perfectly browned in a sputtering butter sauce with a sprinkling of chopped parsley on top. The waiter carefully placed the platter in front of us and stepped back. I closed my eyes and inhaled the rising perfume. Then I lifted a forkful of fish to my mouth, took a bite and chewed slowly. The flesh of the sole was delicate with a light but distinct taste of the ocean that blended marvellously with the browned butter. I chewed slowly and swallowed. It was a morsel of perfection [. . .]'

Write about 200 to 250 words.

Up to 10 marks are available for the content of your answer.

....

....

....

....

....

....

[10]

[Total: 20]

6 Reading practice

Extended response to reading

Re-read **Text C**, *My Life in France*, and then answer **Question 4**.

Question 4

You are Julia Child. After becoming a famous television chef in the USA, you are interviewed for a radio programme about how your interest in French cookery began when you first moved to France. The interviewer asks the following three questions:

- What were your first impressions of the restaurant itself and the service provided by the staff?
- What did you enjoy most about the food you were served?
- What did you learn that day and what impact did it have on your future?

Use your own words to write Julia's responses to each of the interviewer's questions.

Write about 250 to 300 words.

Up to 10 marks are available for reading and up to 10 marks for writing.

....

....

....

....

....

....

....

....

....

....

....

....

....

....

.... [20]

[Total: 20]

> Unit 7
Writing skills

> **LEARNING INTENTIONS**
>
> By the end of this unit, you will be able to:
>
> - write short texts for specific audiences and purposes
> - understand and use different language choices for effect
> - understand and use different sentence types for effect
> - structure texts in different ways
> - practise accurate use of spelling, punctuation and grammar.

7.1 Content and style

1 Match the type of writing with the correct description of content and style. The first one has been done for you.

Type of writing	Content and style
1 a letter to a friend giving advice about career choices	A sequenced, lively events that lead to a happy outcome; accessible rather than formal or challenging language
2 a thank you letter to a teacher	B a series of points that create a logical argument; formal, persuasive language
3 an adventure story for ten-year-olds	C a series of points that create a logical argument; relatively informal language
4 a letter to a newspaper arguing for more money to be spent on education	D appreciative content directed at an audience of one; heartfelt language; formality depends on relationship

(1 matches with C)

2   Match each of these examples of different voices to its correct description.
    The first one has been done for you.

Examples	Type of voice
1 I refuse to believe that you can't give me a refund on this phone. This is the third time I've written to you and it's becoming tiresome.	A excited
2 Mr Frankland was a serious man. Very serious indeed. If only he'd taken time to look in the mirror before leaving the house, he would have seen the traces of egg in his moustache. Had he seen them, he would have been most seriously annoyed.	B comic
3 I can't wait for the next film in the series. It's going to be amazing! The same characters, the same settings, but a whole new story. Bring it on!	C serious
4 The country needs to reflect on its attitudes towards health. The warning signs are there, so ignoring them is reckless. We need a rethink.	D frustrated

    (Example 1 matched to D frustrated)

3   Write three examples of your own in different types of voice.
    You might choose from the voices in Activity 2, or create your own.

    ....

    ....

    ....

    ....

    ....

    ....

    ....

    ....

    ....

    ....

7 Writing skills

....

....

....

....

....

....

....

....

....

....

....

....

....

....

....

....

....

....

....

4 Consider Extracts A and B from thank you letters to teachers. If you wrote a similar letter to your English teacher at the end of the year, which of these two voices would you use and why?

A

> Hi Sir,
>
> Just a quick note to say thanks for teaching me this year.
> I really enjoyed your lessons. I learnt lots and they were fun.

B

> Dear Miss Smith,
>
> I am writing this letter to express my gratitude. Your lessons were stimulating and productive.

....

....

....

....

....

....

5 Write the first paragraph of a letter to a relative thanking them for a present. Start by considering:

- the content of your opening
- how you would address your relative at the start of the letter
- the voice you would adopt
- the formality of the language you would use.

Write around 60 words. Take care with spelling, punctuation and grammar.

....

....

....

....

....

....

....

....

....

7.2 Text structures

6 Events A–F are from the opening section of a children's adventure story. Put the events in order of the time sequence in which you think they would occur.

- **A** Sami finds herself under threat from a malevolent force in the new world which wants the coin.
- **B** As she walks to school, Sami notices something glinting in the grass. She picks it up.
- **C** Sami, a ten-year-old girl, is bored. She longs for something interesting to happen.
- **D** The next morning, Sami's world has changed. She appears to have gone back in time. In her pocket is the gold coin.
- **E** Sami learns that the coin gives special powers to its keeper. Sami appears to be highly powerful in her new world.
- **F** A stranger arrives at Sami's home and demands the return of the coin. Sami has no idea what the man is talking about.

Sequence:

....

7 How could you put the events from Activity 6 in a different order to tell the story in a different way to create different effects? Write your new order below. Explain which version you prefer and why.

New sequence:

....

I prefer ....

....

....

....

8 Here is a basic story outline.

A girl regularly visits her grandmother in hospital. Eventually, her grandmother leaves hospital.

Here is a student's structure plan for the story outline:

> - Emma enters the hospital corridor and wanders to the ward where her grandmother is staying. They chat and Emma returns home.
> - Emma returns the next week. Her grandmother seems a little weaker.
> - When Emma returns the following week, her grandmother has recovered.
> - Emma and her grandmother return home together.

Rewrite this structure plan, adding more detail to engage the reader. For example, you might add another character or start at a different point in the story.

....

....

....

....

....

....

....

....

....

....

9 Choose one of these basic story outlines and write your own structure plan.
- A lonely character eventually finds friendship.
- An ambitious character makes wrong choices and suffers for it.
- A character is put in a dangerous situation but escapes.

....

....

7.3 Word and sentence choices

10 Look at Text 7.1. Select synonyms to replace the words in bold in the text, which are also listed in Table 7.1. Check that your choices make sense in the context of the story, then write your synonyms in Table 7.1.

Text 7.1

> As Amir and Jane **walked** along the **narrow** sandy path, Amir began to **feel** vague anticipation somewhere inside him. The sea was obscured for now though, and all that they could see were tall dune grasses, a seabird pecking at something on the path, and the **huge** grey sky. A **weak** sun drifted high above them, lonely in the emptiness.

Original word	Possible replacements
walked	
narrow	
feel	
huge	
weak	

Table 7.1

11 Which of the possible replacements do you prefer? Underline one preferred replacement for each word in Table 7.1. Before you do, think carefully about the effect your choice would create.

12 The brief outline shown here continues the story from Text 7.1. Write your own version of the story in your notebook, using some interesting words to engage your reader. Write around 80 words.

> Amir and Jane came to the end of the path. They saw the sea.

LANGUAGE FOCUS: SENTENCE TYPES FOR EFFECT

You can achieve interesting effects in your writing through the choice and arrangement of different sentence types. Consider these examples:

- Although Ali tried not to look back, he couldn't help but take a long, last look at the place he called home and as he did so, he shed a silent tear. This was goodbye.

- Creak. Something dark and unknown made its way slowly up the stairs, wheezing as it climbed. Maria cowered.

In the first example, the long, **complex sentence** provides detail about the situation. It also has a sense of rhythm, as if the story is unfolding and the voice is consciously shaping it. The brief **simple sentence** that follows it not only provides contrast but is stark – just like the idea it contains.
The combination of these contrasting sentences helps to emphasise the feeling of sadness in the story.

The second example combines a **minor sentence**, a complex sentence and a simple sentence. The single-word minor sentence is unusual and helps to suggest drama, as if something odd is happening. The complex sentence adds detail to the story, which is nicely complemented by the short, simple sentence at the end, as if the terseness of the final sentence mirrors the terror Maria is feeling.

Remember that 'effects' can sometimes refer to emotional effects on the reader, such as surprise, pity or disgust. Effects can also mean more ordinary effects such as providing detail, contrast or conveying information in a concise way.

KEY TERMS

complex sentence: a sentence that has a main clause and one or more subordinate clauses, introduced by a subordinating conjunction

simple sentence: a sentence that just has one main clause

minor sentence: a sentence that does not contain a main verb

13 Read Text 7.2. Identify one example each of a minor sentence, a simple sentence, a compound sentence (a sentence with more than one verb joined by a coordinating conjunction) and a complex sentence. Copy them into Table 7.2 and explain their effects.

Text 7.2

> The beach was not really that interesting to Amir. It seemed pointless. Car parks had a purpose. Shops had a purpose and sport had a purpose. This was just some sand and salty water, which could look pretty in certain lights, admittedly, but today it was dull. Boring, in fact. It was just a beach. Amir decided it would be better if he kept this thought to himself though, because Jane was currently adopting one of her many yoga poses and he knew from bitter experience that she didn't like being interrupted in such moments.

Sentence	Effect
Minor sentence:	
Simple sentence:	
Compound sentence:	
Complex sentence:	

Table 7.2

14 Redraft your response to Activity 12 in your notebook, changing the types of sentences you have used, aiming to create different effects. As you do so, take care with spelling, punctuation and grammar.

> Unit 8
Directed writing

LEARNING INTENTIONS

By the end of this unit, you will be able to:

- discuss and evaluate opinions
- write articles, reports, letters and speeches, giving opinions
- write for different audiences
- use persuasive language
- use conjunctions to shape a debate
- use colons for effect.

8.1 Evaluating views

1 Read Text 8.1, an extract from an article about the benefits of being bilingual.

Text 8.1

> **Two voices**
>
> Being bilingual means being able to speak two languages. But it means much more than that. When we moved from Australia (the best country in the world) to France (the next best), a great thing happened. My young children learnt to speak French. One of the best things about this was that it helped them to settle into their new country much more quickly. They developed friendships more easily. All children are adaptable, but learning a new language helps with confidence. Older people always struggle to learn new languages, but they too are helped by the process. Research shows that bilingual people tend to be more empathic. They understand others more readily.

Identify three reasons why the writer says being able to speak two languages benefits people.

Reason 1:

....

....

Reason 2:

....

....

Reason 3:

....

....

2   Re-read Text 8.1. Find three facts and three opinions.

Fact 1:

....

....

Fact 2:

....

....

Fact 3:

....

....

Opinion 1:

....

....

Opinion 2:

....

....

Opinion 3:

....

....

3 Now think about who wrote the article.

   a What can you work out about the writer's context (their age, life experiences, attitudes, gender and cultural background)?

   ....

   ....

   ....

   ....

   ....

   ....

   b How might this context have informed their views about speaking two languages?

   ....

   ....

   ....

   ....

   ....

   ....

4 Read Text 8.2, in which a university researcher writes about the challenges of being bilingual. Write down the points of their **argument**.

Text 8.2

> **Twice as hard**
>
> Despite the many benefits of being bilingual, there are some disadvantages. When you only speak one language, you become an expert in it. Bilingual people don't have the same degree of fluency. They generally have a narrower vocabulary in both languages. They also take longer to process what they hear and to react to it. They find it much harder to grasp the subtleties of language, such as its humour. Speaking two languages can also have a slightly odd effect. Many bilingual people often report a sort of personality change when they switch between languages, with one language leading them to be more emotional in the way they express themselves.

> **KEY TERM**
>
> **argument:** a set of reasons in support of a view

....

....

....

....

....

....

5   Evaluate the view of the writer in Text 8.2. Use your own words to comment on the points they have made.

....

....

....

....

....

....

6   Imagine you have been asked to give your own views about the experiences of bilingual people. Using the information from Texts 8.1 and 8.2, explain which points you find most convincing and why.

....

....

....

....

....

....

8.2 Responding to a task

7 Look carefully at Task 8.1, then summarise what it is asking you to do. Explain what the main debate is and what the audience and purpose suggest about language choices.

> **Task 8.1**
>
> Write an article for young people giving your views about whether being bilingual is a positive or negative experience.
>
> ....
>
> ....
>
> ....
>
> ....
>
> ....

8 Read the notes that a student has made summarising the main points from Texts 8.1 and 8.2. Answer the questions to begin shaping your own response to the task.

Text 8.1

- Helps to quickly settle in a new country
- Develops friendships
- Develops confidence
- Makes people more empathic

Text 8.2

- Sometimes lack fluency
- Narrower vocabulary
- Miss the subtleties of language
- Alters personality

a Which points from the texts will you echo in your article?

....

....

....

....

....

b What ideas of your own do you have about the topic?

....

....

....

....

....

c What will your angle be – what view will you take?

....

....

....

....

....

9 Read the start of a student's response to Task 8.1, then look at the list of common errors that are made in directed writing tasks (Table 8.1). Tick the seven errors that the student has made in this response.

> Lots of people is bilingual. It can be a good thing because Text A says that it 'helps with confidence'. I agree with this. It also says old peeple find it hard to learn new languages. Which is right. The other text is also good and makes things true. It says that its can be tough knowing two voices. You can be a different person and you don't know as many words. I agree with that as well.

Common error	Tick
Quoting directly from the texts	
Inappropriate opening	
Analysing the language of the texts	
Unclear phrasing	
Unsuitable register	
Inaccurate spelling	
Limited sentence variety	
Limited personal view given	

Table 8.1

10 Write your own opening to Task 8.1 in your notebook. Write around 120 words. You could start with one of these opening sentences or use one of your own.

- Is there anything more liberating than being able to speak two languages?
- Successful communication is central to our lives.

LANGUAGE FOCUS: ARRANGING COMPLEX SENTENCES

Complex sentences help to organise information and express details. They also provide variety for the reader, adding to the 'rhythm' of a piece of writing in combination with other sentences. Complex sentences consist of a main clause (a group of words that can form a complete sentence) and a subordinate clause (a group of words that only make complete sense alongside a main clause).

Look at this example. The main clause appears second and the subordinate clause appears first.

Although I can understand this to a degree, as I often use technology for research, [2] these things are complex topics, not basic facts. **[1]**

2	subordinate clause

1	main clause

Linking words such as 'although', 'which' and 'because' are often used to connect clauses, and the clauses themselves can often be arranged in different ways. For example:

These things are complex topics, not basic facts, **[1] although I can understand this to a degree, as I often use technology for research. [2]**

1	main clause

2	subordinate clause

Notice that in the first example, placing the main clause at the end provides a more authoritative tone – it concludes the sentence in a strong way. The second example ends in a more conciliatory way, perhaps weakening the point being made.

Using complex sentences accurately in your work displays control of English. However, always think about the arrangement of your clauses and how they can change the impact of the point you are making.

11 Review your response to Activity 10. Rewrite two sections of it using complex sentences.

Rewrite 1:

....

....

....

....

....

....

Rewrite 2:

....

....

....

....

....

....

8.3 Presenting your views

12 You may choose a view because you genuinely believe it, or because you can think of several points to support it. Which of the views in Table 8.2 would you choose to support? Tick the appropriate columns.

View	Agree	Disagree
All town centres should ban all cars and all public transport. It would be better for the public.		
Parents should be able to monitor their children's use of social media. It would lead to fewer problems.		
Every teenager should take on voluntary work at the weekend. It would help young people be more understanding of others' situations.		

Table 8.2

13 Look at points A–E, which all support the view that being bilingual is a positive thing. What do you think would be the best sequence to present these points? You may want to start by identifying the point that you feel would make a good **climax** to your piece.

   A   The world is a far happier place when people from different countries communicate.

   B   Those who speak other languages are more confident.

   C   Different cultures understanding each other leads to tolerance and peace – bilingualism makes for a better world.

   D   Bilingual people have better life chances – they have greater work opportunities and travel more widely.

   E   Bilingual people are more adaptable and can develop wider friendships.

   Best sequence: ....

> **KEY TERMS**
>
> **climax:** the most exciting or important part of something
>
> **rhetorical:** relating to a way of writing or speaking that is designed to influence people

14 Write a sentence using each of the **rhetorical** techniques listed to present a view about whether being bilingual is a positive experience.

   a   a specific example or account

   ....

   ....

   b   a reference from everyday life

   ....

   ....

   c   contrasting attitudes with real-world experiences

   ....

   ....

   d   a positive emotional experience

   ....

   ....

   e   use of listing

   ....

   ....

In Topic 8.2 (Activities 8 and 10), you planned and wrote the opening paragraph to Task 8.1:

> **Task 8.1**
>
> Write an article for young people giving your views about whether being bilingual is a positive or negative experience.

15 Re-read your paragraph, considering the points and techniques you have explored in this section. In your notebook, revise your plan so that it includes better points, an improved sequence and some ideas for using rhetorical techniques.

16 Now write a full response to Task 8.1 in your notebook. Write 250–350 words. Remember to take care with your spelling, punctuation and grammar.

8.4 Writing letters and reports

17 Complete Table 8.3 to suggest appropriate greetings and sign-offs for each scenario. The first one has been done for you.

Audience and purpose	Greeting	Sign-off
A letter to the editor of a national newspaper arguing that more money should be spent on education.	Dear Editor	Yours faithfully
An adult's letter to their old English teacher, thanking them for their help at school.		
A letter to a very close friend who has had some sad news.		
A letter to a large company requesting information about a job.		

Table 8.3

18 Read Text 8.3 aloud, taking care to speak clearly. It is an extract from a blog someone wrote about their life choices. List four benefits that the author has got from their job.

Text 8.3

> **Moving on**
>
> I enjoyed school, but when I had to decide between further study or getting a job, the choice was easy. I got a job. In my opinion, school can only teach you so much about the real world. When I got my job with an IT company, it helped me learn how to talk to and cooperate with others. I feel much more confident now. I feel part of the adult world. I play sport with my colleagues and go for lunch with them. We share a similar sense of humour. The other thing I enjoy is getting paid! It's a great feeling knowing that I'm earning money. Next month, I'm moving into my own house.

....

....

....

....

19 The following student response is from the middle section of a letter to a cousin advising them to stay at school rather than get a job. Highlight and number parts of the text to identify three different features:

1 = where the student has echoed ideas from Text 8.3

2 = where they have used rhetorical techniques

3 = where they have given a strong view

> Is getting a job rather than staying at school such a good idea? It might suit some of your friends, but it wouldn't work for you: you need to have teachers who will push you to excel. Yes, you could earn money in a job, but is that the most important thing in life at the moment? Of course not. I know you could be a brilliant scientist. It's been your passion for so long and there's only one way to do that – further study. Education will be more useful to you in the long run. Staying at school might be an easy option for some people, but in your case, it's not – it's the best way to challenge that brilliant mind of yours.

LANGUAGE FOCUS: COLONS AND DASHES FOR EFFECT

Using more complex punctuation devices, such as the colon, demonstrates your technical skills. Your choice of punctuation should also reflect the style and tone you are trying to create. Look at this example:

- While it might be true for a small minority, I'm not convinced that it is in most students' best interests: having a timetable, a set of rules and a group of teachers who would challenge you is far more beneficial.

Here, the colon introduces the list that follows. It also creates a formal aspect to the writing, especially when the argument is a little more forceful and a 'serious' point is being made.

Dashes are also effective ways to organise a sentence, but they are usually used when a less formal tone is required. Before you make this kind of choice, consider the effect you are trying to achieve at that point in your writing. For example:

- Likewise, learning to accept constructive advice and follow orders – even if I didn't always agree with them! – has served me well.

Here, the dash seems more conversational and fits with the light-hearted tone being used. Less formal punctuation helps the persuasive approach by implying a close relationship between writer and addressee.

You may choose different types of punctuation in different parts of your writing. For instance, in sections where a serious tone is required, colons or semicolons may be the best option.

20 Look again at the student's response in Activity 19. Comment on the use and effect of

   a the colon

       ....

       ....

   b the dashes

       ....

       ....

21 In your notebook, write a paragraph to be included in a report giving reasons why continued education is best for young people. You could use some of the following ideas in your paragraph:

- Students develop expertise in their chosen subjects.
- It is rewarding to study subjects at a more advanced level.
- Better qualifications lead to better jobs.
- Older students develop stronger, supportive relationships with their teachers.

Write around 120 words. Use colons and dashes where appropriate.

8.5 Writing a speech

In Topic 8.4, you looked at the different arguments for and against staying on at school or getting a job. Now read another extract from the blog from Text 8.3.

Text 8.3 (continued)

> You learn something completely different in a job – practical skills. I think that a lot of what you learn at school has very little to do with the real world. I don't think I've used more than 5% of what I learnt when I was in full-time education. At work, the things I learn about IT I use every day. Having a job seems more useful and rewarding than just studying and doing exams. At the end of each day at work, I feel fulfilled – as if I've usually achieved something practical, such as fixing an IT problem. I feel more like an adult now. I like that feeling.

22 What other reasons can you think of for getting a job rather than staying in school? Add your ideas to the following list.

> **Why getting a job is a good idea:**
>
> 1 Improves communication with adults.
>
> 2 Develops confidence.

23 Read Text 8.4, the opening of a student's speech arguing that starting a career is better than staying at school. Highlight and number parts of the text to identify three different features:

1 = where the speaker uses figurative language

2 = where they have used rhetorical techniques

3 = where the speaker addresses the audience directly

Text 8.4

> Good afternoon. Last month, I was at a fork in the road – a point in my life when I needed to choose which route to take. Should I follow the path of education and continue the studies I have enjoyed so much? Or should I take a less familiar route: a new, challenging and slightly daunting one? I spent a lot of time weighing up the possibilities. For some people, further education is an obvious choice; it gives you the opportunity to really understand the subjects that are important to you. Undoubtedly, further study increases your knowledge and the relationships you have with teachers are different – you feel you are treated like an adult. But after careful thought, I chose a different path. I wanted to challenge myself in a new setting. Starting a career was the right thing to do, and I'm going to tell you why it will also be the right thing for you.

24 Read Text 8.4 again. Describe the voice of the text – what clues can you see about their age and the way in which the voice comes across to the audience?

....

....

....

....

Now read Text 8.5, the opening to another speech in which a student argues that staying at school is preferable to starting a career.

Text 8.5

> Good morning. When I was your age, I faced the same choice you are facing: should I continue with my studies or should I enter the world of work? On the one hand, continuing with my studies seemed a natural thing to do. After all, I had spent the past ten years in education, so why would I want to change? I'm sure many of you feel the same way. I also knew there was another choice open to me: starting a career. Some of my friends chose this route and within months, they were earning money and had a wider circle of friends. But then I thought about me. I loved the challenge of fresh academic knowledge and thrived on exams. I viewed education as a fine thing and the mastering of subjects as a joy. This morning, I'm going to explain why continuing with your studies now is the best thing you will ever do.

25 Comment on the voice of this speech.

   a What does it suggest about the speaker's age and experience?

....

....

....

....

....

b Do you prefer the voice in Text 8.4 or Text 8.5? Explain why.

....

....

....

....

26 In your notebook, write the opening section of a speech to young people giving your own view about whether staying at school is worthwhile. Use any of the ideas you have read and thought about based on Texts 8.4 and 8.5. Write around 120 words. Remember to take care with spelling, punctuation and grammar.

Practice questions

Read Texts 8.6 and 8.7 and then complete Activities 27 and 28 to practise your writing.

Text 8.6

> **Challenge yourself**
>
> When I was six, the end of my street was as far as I dared to go. I was brought up in a small town in Sri Lanka. I couldn't have wished for a nicer place to grow up. I moved to Canada when I was 18 to study mathematics. At first, it was like living on the moon. The people were different. The language was different. The landscape was different. It would have been easy to return home, but very soon, I grew to love the place. Studying abroad allows you opportunities that are more than just academic. It's a way to find out more about the world and discover all that the world has to offer. It's a way of challenging yourself to grow as a person. For me, studying abroad showed me that I could rely upon myself rather than my family.
>
> I initially moved to Canada for academic reasons. The university offered a great course and the University of Montreal looked like a great place to learn. I didn't think there was any equivalent university course in my home country. When I started my course, I was so happy with my choice. It was ideal, so right from the start I felt that I'd made the right decision.
>
> When I first arrived in Canada, I quickly had to overcome some language barriers. I spoke English fairly well and knew some French, but the real language that people speak in everyday life was a bit beyond me at first. But being in that situation forced me to learn quickly – and it was such a fantastic experience. It helped me make friends and helped me fit in with the people on my course. That's one of the big benefits of studying overseas: it teaches you how to get along with all types of people. I found out that underneath all the superficial differences, humans are very similar. Living overseas is a great way to learn tolerance and respect for other humans.
>
> Studying abroad is fascinating and it's something everybody should try.

Text 8.7

Life lessons

The decision about where to continue your studies is a difficult one. For some students, the lure of a new life overseas is seductive. For others, an academic experience much closer to home is the right choice. There is, of course, no right answer to this life decision, but it is often the case that studying in your home country is a better option. Doing so allows you to continue your education with the comforting sense of familiarity that home country study brings. Many students report that university life is hard enough without the extra pressure of acclimatising to a new culture. For instance, studying overseas means you need to learn a new language, immerse yourself in a new environment and quickly learn the unwritten rules of the land you choose to move to. All that is in addition to beginning what will be the toughest academic course you have studied so far.

For every student who loves their overseas adventure, there are many more who struggle. They miss the support network of their home country where their families are a train journey away. These students report feeling isolated at times and there are some who return home once the challenges become too much.

Why not investigate the benefits of studying in your home country? There will be universities which are a perfect fit for you. The right course, the right location and the right support systems. Your education is one of the most important things in your life, so make sure you pick a situation that will offer you the best chance of success. Go somewhere where all you need to focus on is studying and making new friends. I spent my university years in a city one hour from my hometown. I enjoyed new freedoms, made new friends and had a very successful time. I think that was because I felt secure. I wasn't expected to learn a new language, and I knew that home was only a short journey away. It felt right for me. Whatever decision you make in the end, make sure it is the right one for you.

27 Re-read this extract from Text 8.6.

> When I was six, the end of my street was as far as I dared to go. I was brought up in a small town in Sri Lanka. I couldn't have wished for a nicer place to grow up. I moved to Canada when I was 18 to study mathematics. At first, it was like living on the moon. The people were different. The language was different. The landscape was different.
>
> It would have been easy to return home, but very soon, I grew to love the place. Studying abroad allows you opportunities that are more than just academic. It's a way to find out more about the world and discover all that the world has to offer. It's a way of challenging yourself to grow as a person. For me, studying abroad showed me that I could rely upon myself rather than my family.

Using your own words, evaluate the writer's attitude towards studying abroad. Give details from the text to justify your answer.

....

....

....

....

.... **[5]**

28 You have been asked to speak to a group of students on the topic of studying abroad. Specifically, you are to present views on the benefits of studying abroad or studying in your home country when you are older.

Use your own words to write your article based on what you have read in both Text 8.6 and Text 8.7.

In your speech, you should:

- discuss different views about the topic
- give your own views about whether young people would benefit more from studying abroad or studying in their home country.

Write about 250 to 350 words.

Up to 10 marks are available for reading and up to 25 marks for writing. **[35]**

29 Now read your speech aloud. Aim to read clearly and fluently.

> Unit 9

Descriptive writing

> **LEARNING INTENTIONS**
>
> By the end of this unit, you will be able to:
> - plan ideas for descriptive writing
> - use figurative language to describe places, events and people
> - use sensory descriptions to develop the content of your writing
> - use different points of view and perspectives
> - write engaging openings and endings
> - make effective language choices
> - practise accurate use of spelling, punctuation and grammar.

9.1 Describing places

1 Effective description relies in part on feelings and atmosphere. What feelings and atmosphere would you create for the following tasks, based on describing places?

   a   Describe walking through a large forest.

   ....

   ....

   ....

   b   Describe a very busy train station.

   ....

   ....

   ....

   c   Describe the view from the top of a hill.

   ....

   ....

   ....

2   Complete Table 9.1, suggesting an event to provide some interest to each of the descriptions. The first one has been done for you.

Task prompt	Minor event and its effect
Describe walking through a large forest.	Event: The narrator comes across a clearing in the forest where some trees have been felled. Effect: The mood is slightly pessimistic as it reveals the negative impact that humans can have on the natural environment.
Describe a very busy train station.	
Describe the view from the top of a hill.	

Table 9.1

> ### LANGUAGE FOCUS: METAPHOR, SIMILE AND PERSONIFICATION
>
> Simile and metaphor are both ways of making comparisons. They also help to extend meanings and ideas. Consider this simile:
>
> - . . . its houses standing like guards.
>
> This creates an image of strength and security, but there is also the implication that the place requires protection – as if there are threats lurking.
>
> Metaphor operates in a similar way. It helps the reader to understand situations as well as the feelings and qualities attached to them. Consider this metaphor, which describes a storm:
>
> - . . . it ended in a crescendo of hate.
>
> In this musical metaphor, the reader learns that the storm builds to a loud climax. The word 'hate' suggests its aggressive nature and gives a sense of threat.
>
> Another form of figurative language is personification, where inanimate objects are given human qualities. Here is an example:
>
> - The wind, a quiet stranger, strolled the morning streets.
>
> This use of personification helps the reader to understand the presence of the wind in the town and its superficially unthreatening nature. However, the comparison to a 'stranger' also suggests something unknown and makes the reader wonder whether the wind's presence might cause problems.

3 For each of the following sentences, identify the technique used (simile, metaphor or personification) and describe its effect.

   a His anger was like a monster, its tentacles lashing out in fury.

   Technique: ....

   Effect: ....

   ....

   b The tall buildings loomed over me.

   Technique: ....

   Effect: ....

   ....

   c The sun was my mother, caressing and giving life to me.

   Technique: ....

   Effect: ....

   ....

4 Write a paragraph of around 60 words describing a visit to a remote island. Start by thinking about the feelings and atmosphere you want to create and choose suitable figurative language to convey them.

9.2 Describing details

5 Read Text 9.1, in which the writer describes the scenery in Umbria. Highlight the adjectives.

Text 9.1

> Umbria in January is smoky and blue. The rosebushes are bare. Dead leaves rattle in the oaks… An hour after dawn it begins to snow. It tinkles on the branches and the woodpile like shavings of glass. The valley below the house is a brilliant white; three soft lights glow far below us. The sun comes up and sets the hills on fire [. . .] Time is larger here. Hawks come over the house and frost whitens the mulberries.
>
> from *Four Seasons in Rome* by Anthony Doerr

6 Comment on the effect of the following uses of figurative language to describe the details of the scene.

    a 'It tinkles on the branches and the woodpile like shavings of glass.'

    ....

    ....

    b 'The sun comes up and sets the hills on fire.'

    ....

    ....

7 Choose an outdoor place you know well, such as a place you regularly visit or the street where you live. Write three sentences describing features of the place.
You might describe buildings, natural objects or human-made objects.
Try to capture the details through adjective choices and / or figurative language.

Sentence 1: ....

....

....

Sentence 2: ....

....

....

Sentence 3: ....

....

8 Plan to build your sentences into a longer paragraph of around 100 words. Start by completing the mind map. Your plan must include:

  - the overall feeling or atmosphere you are trying to create
  - a minor event you will include
  - further specific details you will include, such as objects, sights and sounds.

Describe an outdoor place you know well

9 In your notebook, write your paragraph of around 100 words. Focus on using effective word choices to describe the details of the place. Start by considering what effective adjectives and figurative language you might use.

9.3 Using the senses

> **LANGUAGE FOCUS: SENSORY DESCRIPTIONS**
>
> The human senses of sight, hearing, touch, smell and taste are often used in composition writing.
>
> You can use visual descriptions to refer to what can be seen. For example:
>
> - The street food stall was an old shack on the side of the road.
>
> Use auditory descriptions to refer to what can be heard. When combined with visual descriptions, they can bring a scene to life for your reader. For example:
>
> - The old street food vendor yelled to sell his produce, his voice shrill and grating.
>
> Tactile descriptions refer to things related to the sense of touch.
> This means not only what can be sensed by the hands but by the whole body. For example:
>
> - The warmth of the food brought life back to my cold fingers.
> - The rain fell heavily as we ate, my body shivering from the cold.
>
> You will probably use olfactory descriptions (relating to smell) and gustatory descriptions (relating to taste) less frequently, but they can also be very effective. For example:
>
> - The smell of onions being fried in the open air was delightful.
> - The sweet taste of freshly cooked dumplings exploded in my mouth.

10 Read Text 9.2, a short description set in a hotel room. In Table 9.2, list the references to sights, sounds and touch.

Text 9.2

> In flickering light, my eyes traced the cracks on the ceiling. I was helplessly falling into sleep after a long day's travel. Somewhere downstairs, a monotonous clock, like a mother's gentle lullaby, was beckoning me to sleep. I'd soon surrender.
>
> The wind outside played a melancholy tune as it whistled through the ivy that covered the front of the hotel. There was music in the night: the howl of a fox somewhere in the hills; the rhythmic crunch of gravel; the hushed melody of a late-night arrival.
>
> Earlier today, the sunlight had peered over the hills and touched the face of the hotel. The lush greenery softened its forbidding glare and once inside, I felt home. Day turned into evening and sleep awaited.

> The music of the night was drawing to a close: the gentle swish of curtains next door; the soft closing of a lock; the fading hum of air conditioning. Tomorrow, I'd travel onwards. But for now, I was safe. Safe in my hotel, caressed by cotton sheets, my limbs weary and my mind floating off.
>
> In flickering light, my eyes traced the cracks on the ceiling. I was helplessly falling into sleep.
>
> I surrendered.

Sights	Sounds	Touch

Table 9.2

11 Think about the room you are sitting in now. What can you sense?
Write three sentences. One should refer to sight, one to sound and one to touch.
Use figurative language where appropriate.

Sentence 1:

....

....

....

Sentence 2:

....

....

....

Sentence 3:

....

....

....

12 Complete a mind map like the one in Figure 9.1 to start planning a description of the room you are in using your sense impressions. (You may not be able to include points about the sense of taste.)

```
                      This room
           /      /      |      \      \
       Sight   Smell   Taste   Touch   Sound
```

Figure 9.1

13 In your notebook, write a description of the room you are in, using your plan.
Use sense description, figurative language and interesting word choices.
You might invent some extra details to add some interest. Write around 150 words.

9.4 Describing events

14 Look at Task 9.1, an event-based task.

> **Task 9.1**
>
> Describe an unusual encounter.

What event could you include in a response to this task? Two suggestions have been provided. Add two more suggestions to the list. As you do so, take care with spelling, punctuation and grammar.

- A person comes across an unusual animal.

- Two people from different parts of the world share a train journey.

- ....

- ....

15 Complete Table 9.3, giving different examples of opening sentences.
The first one has been done for you as an example.

Approach	Example
Focus on a specific place	The train left the busy Cape Town station.
Focus on the weather	
Focus on scenery	
Focus on touch	
Focus on feelings	

Table 9.3

16 Choose one of these approaches and write the opening paragraph in response to the task in your notebook.

- Decide what will happen during the unusual encounter.
- Plan the atmosphere and sense descriptions you will include.
- Write in the third-person voice.
- Write around 100 words.

17 Here is a student's response to Task 9.1. Summarise its effectiveness, commenting on how well it:

- prepares the reader for the accident that is about to happen
- describes the sights, sounds and feelings of the scene.

> **The streets of Cape Town**
>
> The feeling of anxiety rose up from nowhere. I knew before it happened that something was going to occur. The narrow side streets of Cape Town, which are a riot of colour and people, are not large enough to accommodate bicycles, and yet that morning, a bicycle unsteadily weaved its way along the misshapen pavement. As it came closer, I saw an old man perched on its trembling frame. He veered from one side of the narrow street to the other like a broken shopping trolley beyond its user's control.

....

....

....

....

....

....

....

....

....

....

18 In your notebook, rewrite your response to Activity 16 in the first person. Try to bring out more of the feelings and attitudes you might experience.

9.5 Describing people

19 Read Text 9.3 and make notes on the following features of the extract.

    a The details of Glen's clothing in paragraph 1, and what they suggest about him.

....

....

....

....

....

....

    b What Glen does in paragraph 2 that suggests his personality.

....

....

....

....

....

....

Text 9.3

> The room was cool and smelled of damp concrete, so I opened the wooden shutters to let in the late afternoon sunshine and the salty sea breeze. Through the window I could see Glen, sitting on a wooden swing that he had suspended from the branches of a sturdy tree, swinging gently back and forth with his ankles neatly crossed... He wore a pink polo shirt, knee-length checked shorts and the kind of sports socks that are carefully designed to be only just visible above the top of your trainers. As I walked out of my room, Glen bounced onto his toes from the swing and walked towards me through the sand...

9 Descriptive writing

> It was a Saturday evening and some of the families from the village had come down to the beach to sit together on the sand and watch the sun set over the sea. Glen wandered out onto the beach, talking into a laptop, which he turned to the horizon so the person could see the orange ball of the sun falling from the violet sky.
>
> from 'The Teardrop Island' by Cherry Briggs

20 Write two more sentences to describe Glen as he walks back across the sand. Include details to bring him to life, such as his manner of walking or other actions.

....

....

....

....

....

....

LANGUAGE FOCUS: CHOOSING EFFECTIVE VERBS

Verbs are powerful tools for describing characters. They can help your reader picture how a person moves, acts and speaks, and can convey a character precisely the way you want. For example, the verb 'walked' may show what a character is doing, but it is not very descriptive:

- Sarah walked into the room.

Other verbs would have more power and impact, and reveal more information about the character. For example:

- Sarah strode into the room. (This might suggest that the character is powerful and confident.)
- Sarah glided into the room. (This might suggest that the character moves gracefully.)
- Sarah sneaked into the room. (This might suggest that the character is entering the room without permission.)

When you describe a character, always look at your verb choices and decide if you should select a more effective verb.

21 Read the following passage and write suitable verbs in the gaps to show Samira's actions and feelings.

It was 7 p.m. on a warm Madrid evening when Samira .... out of the taxi. As she did so, the hem of her skirt got caught in the car door.

The taxi started to move. Samira .... on the car window and .... The taxi driver didn't hear her.

The taxi started to move a bit faster. With one hand, she

.... the handle of the car door. The other hand

.... her bag. Suddenly, the driver realised what was

happening and braked fiercely. Samira .... to a halt and

....

Practice question

22 In your notebook, write a response to the following practice question:

Describe a young person leaving home.

Write about 350 to 450 words.

Up to 16 marks are available for the content and structure of your answer and up to 24 marks for the style and accuracy of your writing. [40]

9.6 Improving descriptive writing

Read Text 9.4. The narrator is describing flying home after a long journey exploring Pakistan.

Text 9.4

> The helicopter seemed to take an age to ascend, but soon we were weaving between mountains, the bright sunlight catching the snow-covered passes. The statue-like mountains remained unimpressed by my departure. They would still be here after I was gone, and should I return, their impassive faces would still dominate. I turned to take my last view of this beautiful place and then faced forward, ready for a different adventure.

23 Write a paragraph explaining what feelings Text 9.4 leaves you with and why it is an effective ending.

....

....

....

....

....

....

....

....

24 Here is the last paragraph of a student's response to Activity 13 in Topic 9.3, describing the room they are sitting in. Choose three sentences from the response and rewrite them to make them more effective.

> Music is coming from the wireless speaker next to my bed. It's very loud and makes me feel energetic. The sound shakes the windows. It helps me work. Once I've completed homework, I unzip my bag, which sits in the corner of my room, and put my book inside. I switch the light off and walk downstairs.

Sentence 1:

....

....

....

Sentence 2:

....

....

....

Sentence 3:

....

....

....

25 Look back at the response you wrote to Activity 22 in Topic 9.5, where you described a young person leaving home. Rewrite the ending aiming to improve the ideas and word choices. Make sure the ending brings your description 'to a rest'.

26 Using what you have learnt during this unit, write eight top tips for effective descriptive writing.

1 ....

....

2 ....

....

3 ....

....

4 ....

....

5 ....

....

6 ....

....

7 ....

....

8 ....

....

Unit 10
Narrative writing

> **LEARNING INTENTIONS**
>
> By the end of this unit, you will be able to:
>
> - generate story ideas and write plans
> - create engaging characters and settings
> - write effective story openings and endings
> - structure narratives in different ways
> - use a range of language techniques to engage the reader
> - practise accurate use of spelling, punctuation and grammar.

10.1 Story elements and ideas

1. Complete Table 10.1 to show how you could develop familiar story ideas. The first one has been done for you.

Story opening	How it could develop	Possible ending
A An ambitious businessman desires power. He is offered an opportunity to take over the company he works for but will have to do something he doesn't feel comfortable with.	He decides to act and with others, plots to have the current boss sacked. He invents lies that force the boss to resign, then takes over his job. The businessman turns out to be a terrible leader. He rules his company by fear. He is corrupted by power and breaks rules.	His lies begin to come to light. Gradually, his allies desert him. The police discover his corrupt business practices. He is prosecuted and jailed.
B The main character, a teenage girl, is incredibly talented at sport. Her family has no interest in her and she seems destined for an unhappy life.		
C A skilled climber sets off to climb a mountain. She ignores warnings about the dangers she faces, thinking her skill and experience will protect her.		

Table 10.1

2   Highlight the conflict in each story idea in Table 10.1.

3   Look at this list of narrative **genres**.

> Tragedy: where a character suffers and the story ends unhappily.

> Thriller: where the main character faces and survives some dangerously exciting events.

> Romance: where characters discover love, undergo some challenges but the story ends happily.

> Science fiction: where events occur in worlds where technology has advanced significantly.

KEY TERM

genre: a 'type' of story, such as comedy, tragedy or mystery

Choose Story B or C from your completed version of Table 10.1. Then, choose one genre: tragedy, thriller, romance or science fiction. Explain how the story and its main conflict might develop and end if you wrote it in this genre.

....

....

....

....

....

....

10.2 Story openings

Read Text 10.1, then complete Activity 4.

Text 10.1

> **Mountain retreat**
>
> The sun cast a red sheen over Dubai, its gaze catching the peaks of the serene skyscrapers that kept watch over the city's inhabitants. The sun also invaded Khalifa's room, which occupied the top floor of an apartment, where she sat, furrow-browed and tense, as she re-read (for the tenth time) the email that had arrived at dawn. It wasn't a work email. Far from it.
> It was a personal email, and it was one that forced Khalifa into a terrible choice. Whatever choice she made, it could only end badly. Very badly.

4 a Summarise what you learn about the setting from this opening.

....

....

....

....

....

....

b Explain what intrigues the reader most about this opening and why.

....

....

....

....

....

5 Look at the different sentence types in Text 10.1.

    a Use different-coloured highlighters to identify the following sentence types: minor, simple, compound, complex.

    b Choose one sentence from the text and explain why it is effective.

....

....

....

....

6 Write an opening in which you engage your reader. Use different sentence types for effect. Write around 80 words. As you do so, take care with spelling, punctuation and grammar. Use the following story outline or an idea of your own.

A man returns home from work to find a letter has arrived. He opens the letter and is overjoyed at what it says.

....

....

....

....

....

....

....

....

....

10.3 Characterisation

7 Read Text 10.2. As you read, highlight the things that the main character does, feels and thinks.

Text 10.2

> He sat exhausted against a tree trunk, his dark blue shirt wet with sweat. The expanse around him expressed total dryness. He stared at the tufts of dull grass and bits of straw spinning in a column to the sky. The whirlwind sucked brown earth up into the air. He recalled the old people had told him this was a portent of drought, want, disaster, and death, and he was afraid. He was now anxious to get home; he could already see the tips of the bamboo thickets surrounding the house far ahead like blades of glass. But he hesitated. A moment before reaching the shade of the tree he felt his ears buzz and his eyes blur and he knew it meant giddiness and sunstroke. He looked at the soles of his feet blistered from the burning sandy ground and became indescribably angry – angry at the weather capable of such endless torture.
>
> From 'The Gold-Legged Frog' by Khamsing Srinawk

8 Look at the information you have highlighted. Summarise your overall impression of the character, and your reaction to him.

....

....

....

....

....

....

> CAMBRIDGE IGCSE™ FIRST LANGUAGE ENGLISH: WORKBOOK

LANGUAGE FOCUS: DIALOGUE

Dialogue is an effective way to reveal character by showing what someone says and how they say it. It is also a good way to advance a story – key information can be revealed through dialogue.

Consider these two versions of the same event from a thriller story:

Version A

James confronted Montgomery and told him he wouldn't get away with things. Montgomery looked at James and said nothing. Finally, he laughed and told him he didn't care.

Version B

'There's no escape now. Your time is up,' said James triumphantly, as he looked across the ravine at Montgomery. Montgomery stood still until finally a huge laugh shook his frame.

'Tell somebody who cares,' bellowed Montgomery.

Although both versions describe the same event, they have different effects.

Version A reports what is said in a very direct way. This approach can be effective in the climax of a story where brevity is often required.

Version B tells the reader precisely what is said and reveals the way some of those words are spoken. The use of **speech tags** (e.g. 'said James triumphantly', 'bellowed Montgomery'[1]) can suggest characters' personalities and emotions.

When using dialogue in your narrative, it is important to punctuate it accurately. Remember to:

- put a new speaker on a new line
- put the words spoken inside speech marks
- capitalise the first letter inside the speech marks
- include a punctuation mark such as a comma, full stop or exclamation mark before the closing speech mark.

KEY TERMS

dialogue: conversation between two or more people or characters, written as direct speech

speech tag: the verb and / or adverb used to describe the way characters speak in direct speech

[1] In these examples, 'triumphantly' and 'bellowed' are speech tags.

9 In Text 10.3, an extract from the same story, the writer uses dialogue to show the characters of the children. Explain what impression the dialogue gives you of the children and their attitude towards their father.

....

....

....

....

....

Text 10.3

> The two children on either side of him shivered as they stopped to look for frogs hiding in the cracks of the parched earth. Each time they saw two bright eyes in a deep crack, they would shout, 'Pa, here's another one. Pa, this crack has two. Gold-legged ones! Hurry, Pa.'
>
> From 'The Gold-Legged Frog' by Khamsing Srinawk

10 Write a paragraph of around 80 words containing dialogue.
Make sure you punctuate it accurately and choose any speech tags carefully.
Use the following story outline or an idea of your own.

Two young people are in a busy city. One wants to return home.
One wants to stay longer in the city.

....

....

....

....

....

....

....

....

....

....

10.4 Improving narrative structure

11 Read the following plan for a story called 'The repair'. Annotate the plan, identifying the four phases of this **chronological** narrative: exposition, complication, climax and resolution.

> **KEY TERM**
>
> **chronological:** where events occur in time order

> **The repair – story plan**
>
> A father and his grown-up daughter have a difficult relationship. They like each other but tend to argue. One day, they travel together to visit a sick relative. Neither is looking forward to it. It's a long journey and they drive through the night. The car breaks down on a deserted road. They unfairly blame each other. The father telephones for help and as they wait, they argue furiously about things that happened in the past. Ultimately, the argument has a positive effect. They finally begin to listen to each other and as dawn breaks, it seems that their relationship is beginning to improve. Their car is repaired and they drive on, laughing about their silly behaviour.

12 Summarise what happens in each phase.

Exposition:

....

....

Complication:

....

....

Climax:

....

....

Resolution:

....

....

13 Suggest an idea for a **flashback** that could be added to 'The repair' and where it could be added in the storyline. For example, you might suggest an incident from the past that helps to explain the father and daughter's difficult relationship.

....

....

....

....

> **KEY TERMS**
>
> **flashback:** a part of the story set in a time earlier than the main story
>
> **tension:** the feeling that something terrible is about to happen

14 Read Text 10.4, in which a snake threatens baby Artie. Highlight the words that help to create **tension**. Annotate the text to explain **why** these words are effective.

Text 10.4

> An uninvited guest had arrived, a black creature with red and yellow stripes. It moved across the floor. It slithered. Gem whimpered. She didn't know a lot about nature but knew this to be a coral snake. She also knew its potency.
>
> His daughter's stifled tears had roused Kelvin from his sleep. Blinking, he immediately saw the danger. They both did. They in watched in mute horror as the snake made its way across the floor.
>
> It was slowly moving towards Artie, Gem's baby brother, who was sleeping in his basket by the fireplace.

15 In your notebook, write a paragraph of around 100 words where you create tension by placing characters in a risky situation. Use words carefully to help convey tension. You could base your writing on the following story prompt or use an idea of your own.

A dangerous animal is wandering around a town.

10.5 Refining your storytelling

Look at Task 10.1.

> **Task 10.1**
>
> Write a story that involves an upsetting situation.

16 Read the sample answer to Task 10.1 and annotate it to identify the following:
- the emotionally engaging moments
- where the initial problem is introduced
- parts where the characters' actions help to show their attitudes
- where dialogue is used
- where and how well tension is created.

The hospital

We walked down the hospital corridor again. I looked at my mother and father as we walked silently down those long, white passages. My dad was deep in thought and my mother looked like she hadn't slept. We were all worried. My grandmother had been in hospital for two weeks now and we had visited her every day. I just hoped she would come home soon, but none of us really thought that was likely.

Before we entered the ward, a doctor stopped us. He was tall and had a serious face. He told us that he'd like to speak to all of us together soon and that he would come to my grandmother's bed. My father thanked him and the doctor walked off quickly down the long corridor. I could see tears starting to form in my mother's eyes, so I held her hand and we went through the door and into the ward.

My grandmother was sleeping. She looked old and frail. We sat quietly and didn't really know what to say to each other. Before long, the doctor reappeared.

'Your grandmother is fine,' he said. 'She can go home.'

We looked at each other and smiled. It was great news. We had been fearing the worst. My grandmother woke up. She must have sensed our happiness. Once she was dressed, we took her home.

17 The student has redrafted the third paragraph of 'The hospital'.
Read the second draft and answer the following questions.

a What is the effect of the description of the grandmother?

....

....

....

....

b What is the effect of the description of the doctor's and nurses' behaviour?

....

....

....

....

> **The hospital (second draft)**
>
> I looked on in silence at my beautiful grandmother, sleeping. Her thin, grey hair was swept back over her face and her breathing was laboured. I saw the doctor at the other end of the ward. He looked across but neither smiled nor acknowledged us. It seemed to me that time was slowing down and the nurses all knew something.

18 Make a story plan for the following question.

Write a story that involves a difficult choice.

Remember to focus on a dramatic or emotionally engaging moment.
Your plan should include information about:
- the central character
- the time and place setting
- the conflict or problem
- a list of the main events, including the ending.

....

....

....

....

Practice question

19 Write a story that involves a difficult choice.

Write about 350 to 450 words.

Up to 16 marks are available for the content and structure of your answer and up to 24 marks for the style and accuracy of your writing. **[40]**

10.6 Endings

20 In Topic 10.4, you read a plan for a story called 'The repair'.
Read the first idea for the ending (first draft) and then the new version (second draft). Explain which one you find most engaging and why.

> **The repair (first draft)**
>
> Ultimately, the argument has a positive effect. They finally begin to listen to each other and as dawn breaks, it seems that their relationship is beginning to improve. Their car is repaired and they drive on, laughing about their silly behaviour.

> **The repair (second draft)**
>
> They argue like never before, becoming increasingly animated until the daughter leaves the car and walks off down the road. The father is sad but accepts the situation. They never see or speak to each other again.

21 What messages arise from each ending?

Ending 1:

....

....

....

....

....

....

Ending 2:

....

....

....

....

....

....

22 Read the ending of the story you wrote in Topic 10.5. In your notebook, write an alternative ending in which things turn out differently for the characters.

23 Compare the two different story endings you have written. Which one do you prefer and why?

....

....

....

....

....

....

Unit 11
Writing practice

Directed writing

Read **Text A** and **Text B** and then answer **Question 1a and 1b**.

Text A: The way forward

When the digital age began, it was widely assumed that by the 21st century, schools would be places where technology was used to improve education. It hasn't quite happened that way. Perhaps many educators are – inexplicably – reluctant to embrace AI.

AI is, in my view, the way forward. I urge school leaders to think of the potential benefits of AI in the classroom. No teacher wants to spend countless hours marking essays and tests, so why not take advantage of currently available software that can mark and assess students' work in a matter of seconds? Technology speeds up the whole process while getting rid of human inaccuracy and bias. The benefit for teachers is obvious – they would have much more time to do the things that really help students. For students, this means fast, reliable feedback.

When used appropriately, AI can supplement the work teachers do. It can be used to spot patterns in a student's work, identify common errors, design a suitable set of exercises to help them and then reassess in real time. It can even write full textbooks targeted at individual students, or design new exam papers and model answers. AI could be especially helpful for students with specific needs and challenges for whom teachers don't always have the time in a crowded day to provide one-to-one assistance.

There are situations where AI can completely replace teachers, too, using carefully programmed algorithms to suit different learners' needs. Done properly, it would mean that students wouldn't necessarily have to attend a physical school – they could learn from the comfort of their own homes. What's more, they could determine when they want to learn rather than be constrained by a timetable.

Understandably, the concept of AI teaching seems to be a bold step for some educators, but the technology is available and is impossible to ignore. The truth is that once students leave school, they enter a world of work where AI is central, so why not introduce them to its benefits while they're still of school age?

Text B: The value of humans

Education is a profoundly human experience. The process of learning consists of intellectual, social and emotional challenges. And that is why, for centuries, human beings have been at the heart of it. There's no substitute for young people being in the company of an experienced, caring adult who interacts with them, challenges them, supports them and ultimately shapes them into creative and rounded young adults. Education is not just about learning things and testing them; it's a complex, mysterious process that is so much more than being fed worksheets by some faceless computer.

The spectre of AI has hovered over education for a while now. Its supporters tell us that it can reduce teachers' workloads and design educational material to support all students. As a teacher, I can see how a programme that marks books and tests sounds appealing, but is that really what will help students? Perhaps this could work in some subjects, where there are definitively right and wrong answers, but what about subjects like English literature? How could AI possibly assess complex ideas and give accurate feedback? Students need human teachers who understand the nuances of students' work and can help them to see ways to refine things.

The problem with the creep of AI into education is that it dehumanises things. Remote learning sounds briefly exciting, but it is not how humans operate. We're social beings who require interaction with others, often in the same physical space. We need other people to understand us and joke with us, help us and support us. Most of our best memories of school are about human interaction – a funny moment, a favourite teacher, a school show. AI can't give you those moments. But humans can. And they can push you to academic brilliance, too.

Question 1

a Re-read this extract from **Text A**.

'When used appropriately, AI can supplement the work teachers do. It can be used to spot patterns in a student's work, identify common errors, design a suitable set of exercises to help them and then reassess in real time. It can even write full textbooks targeted at individual students, or design new exam papers and model answers. AI could be especially helpful for students with specific needs and challenges for whom teachers don't always have the time in a crowded day to provide one-to-one assistance.'

Use your own words to evaluate the writer's attitude towards the use of AI in schools. Give details from the text to justify your answer. [5]

b Imagine your school is considering making more use of AI for educational purposes. Write a letter to your headteacher explaining whether you think this would be a positive change.

Use your own words to write your letter based on what you have read in both Text A and Text B.

In your letter, you should:

- outline the different attitudes towards the use of AI in education
- give your own views about how AI might affect your experience of education.

Write about 250 to 350 words.

Up to 10 marks are available for reading and up to 25 marks for writing. **[35]**

[Total: 40]

Composition

Write about 350 to 450 words on **one** of the following questions:

Up to 16 marks are available for the content and structure of your answer and up to 24 marks for the style and accuracy of your writing.

EITHER

Descriptive writing

2   Describe a very beautiful place. [40]

OR

3   Write a description with the title 'The sun rising'. [40]

OR

Narrative writing

4   Write a story with the title 'The envelope'. [40]

OR

5   Write a story that involves a happy event. [40]

Glossary

active voice: where the subject of a sentence is the person or thing performing the action

argument: a set of reasons in support of a view

chatty language: the type of language and vocabulary you would use when talking to family or a close friend about unimportant things

chronological: where events occur in time order

climax: the most exciting or important part of something

complex sentence: a sentence that has a main clause and one or more subordinate clauses, introduced by a subordinating conjunction

connotations: the ideas, feelings and associations that a particular word evokes in a reader, in addition to the main meaning of the word

conventions: the 'rules' of how a story is told or a piece of writing is set out

coordinating conjunction: a word such as 'and', 'but', 'or' that joins two words or two main clauses in a sentence

dialogue: conversation between two or more people or characters, written as direct speech

direct speech: the exact words a person says, marked by speech marks

figurative language: words and phrases used not with their basic meaning but with a more imaginative meaning to create a special effect; figurative language techniques include simile, metaphor and personification

flashback: a part of the story set in a time earlier than the main story

genre: a 'type' of story, such as comedy, tragedy or mystery

imply: to suggest something in an indirect way, without stating it explicitly

infer: to work out a meaning by applying evidence and reasoning

metaphor: a type of comparison that describes one thing as if it were something else

minor sentence: a sentence that does not contain a main verb

passive voice: where the verb is placed before the person or thing, so the verb acts upon the subject

personification: a type of figurative language in which an object is described as if it has human characteristics

perspective: the 'angle' that a story or account is told from – whose 'eyes' the reader sees it through

register: the level of formality in a piece of writing

reported speech: a speaker's words reported rather than stated directly, using changes of person and tense and governed by a reporting verb (e.g. 'he **said**', 'she **stated**')

rhetorical: relating to a way of writing or speaking that is designed to influence people

scan: to read a text quickly to locate specific information in it

sensory image: an image that appeals to the reader's senses: sight, sound, touch, taste and smell

simile: a type of figurative language in which one thing is compared to something else using the words 'as' or 'like'

simple sentence: a sentence that just has one main clause

skimming: to read a text quickly to get a general overview of the topic and content

speech tag: the verb and / or adverb used to describe the way characters speak in direct speech

subordinate clause: in grammar, a clause that cannot form a sentence alone but adds information to the main clause

synthesise: to combine or draw together similar points

tension: the feeling that something terrible is about to happen

voice: the personality and attitude of the narrator

> Acknowledgements

The authors and publishers acknowledge the following sources of copyright material and are grateful for the permissions granted. While every effort has been made, it has not always been possible to identify the sources of all the material used, or to trace all copyright holders. If any omissions are brought to our notice, we will be happy to include the appropriate acknowledgements on reprinting.

Unit 3 Text extract from 'Mobile phones in school: Why our rule is 'Meet, Feet, Eat'' by Tomas Duckling, 24 October 2023 www.tes.com; **Unit 4** Abridged extracts from 'Wet, Wet, Wet' by William Gray published by and used with the permission of Wanderlust Travel Media Limited; Extract from 'The Other Side of the Hill' by Ted Hughes from *Poetry in the Making*, used by the permission of Faber & Faber Ltd and Farrar Straus & Giroux; Abridged extract from *Hullabaloo in the Guava Orchard* by Kiran Desai, used by the permission of Faber & Faber Ltd; **Unit 5** Extract from *Fire on the Mountain* by Anita Desai; Abridged extract from 'Trailing the Snow Leopard in Moutainous Ladakh' by Lizzie Pook for The Evening Standard, January 2020, used by the permission of ESI Media; **Unit 6** Excerpt(s) adapted from *MY LIFE IN FRANCE* by Julia Child with Alex Prud'homme, copyright © 2006 by the Julia Child Foundation for Gastronomy and the Culinary Arts and Alex Prud'homme. Used by permission of Alfred A. Knopf, an imprint of the Knopf Doubleday Publishing Group, a division of Penguin Random House LLC. All rights reserved; **Unit 9** Abridged extracts from *Four Seasons in Rome* by Anthony Doerr, Reprinted by permission of HarperCollins Publishers Ltd © 2017.; Abridged extracts from *The Teardrop Island*, by Cherry Briggs, 2013, used by the permission of Summersdale Publishers Ltd.; **Unit 10** Abridged extracts from 'The Gold-legged frog' translated by Domnern Garden from *The Politician and Other Stories*, Silkworm Books

Thanks to the following for permission to reproduce images:

Cover pchyburrs/GI; *Inside* **Unit 1** Andresr/GI; Björn Lauer/GI; **Unit 2** Westend61- Gerald Nowak/GI; Tobias Titz/GI; Richard Newstead/GI; **Unit 3** Taiyou Nomachi/GI; Rudy Sulgan/GI; SolStock/GI; **Unit 4** Alfons Salmhofer/GI; Danny Lehman/GI; Mayur Kakade/GI; Ake1150sb/GI; Aphithana Chitmongkolthong/GI; **Unit 5** Izzet Keribar/GI; Kathleen Reeder Wildlife Photography/GI; **Unit 6** John Elk/GI; **Unit 7** Colin Roberts/GI; Joanne Hedger/GI; **Unit 8** Oko_SwanOmurphy/GI; MesquitaFMS/GI; Sadeugra/GI; FatCamera/GI; **Unit 9** Jose Antonio Maciel/GI; @ Didier Marti/GI; **Unit 10** Westend61/GI; Stuart Gleave/GI; Andrew M. Snyder/GI

Key: GI = Getty Images